BASIC
TECHNICAL
ENGLISH

BASIC TECHNICAL ENGLISH

Jeremy Comfort, Steve Hick, Allan Savage

Oxford University Press

Oxford University Press
Walton Street, Oxford OX2 6DP

Oxford New York
Athens Auckland Bangkok Bombay
Calcutta Cape Town Dar es Salaam Delhi
Florence Hong Kong Istanbul Karachi
Kuala Lumpur Madras Madrid Melbourne
Mexico City Nairobi Paris Singapore
Taipei Tokyo Toronto

and associated companies in
Berlin Ibadan

OXFORD and OXFORD ENGLISH are
trade marks of Oxford University Press

ISBN 0 19 457382 6

© Oxford University Press 1982

First published 1982
Fourteenth impression 1995

The authors wish to thank the following
for their help:

Professor H.G. Widdowson, Institute of
Education, University of London
Dr Farnworth, Head of Engineering
Department, York College of Arts and
Technology
York Language Training Associates Ltd

Illustrations by the Technical Graphics
Department, Oxford University Press.

The publishers would like to thank the
following for permission to reproduce
photographs:

Black and Decker Ltd
Ford Motor Company Ltd
Harland and Wolff Ltd
T.S. Harrison and Sons Ltd
Neill Tools Ltd

Filmset in Lasercomp Calvert by
Filmtype Services Limited, Scarborough,
North Yorkshire

Printed in Hong Kong

Contents

Unit	Page	Topic	Example
1	1	Shapes Forms of transport	squares, circles, etc. bikes, planes, etc.
2	4	Vehicle components	gear boxes, engines, generators, batteries
3	6	Materials	chemical compounds and elements; metals and alloys
4	9	Geometric shapes Rotary systems	cubes, cylinders, etc. gears, pulleys, etc.
5	13	Geometric shapes Electric circuits	pipes, cylinders, etc. resistance
6	16	Rotary systems Drills Cameras	gears wood and metal
7	21	Cutting tools and machines Vehicle components	chisels, lathes and milling machines cylinder blocks, sumps, axles, etc.
8	25	Manual operations Generators Petrol engines	jacks, levers, etc. fan belt adjustment piston function
9	29	Manual controls Rotary systems	taps, buttons, etc. cranes, pulleys, cooling and lubricating systems
10	32	Valves	canals, water tanks, petrol engines
11	36	Measuring instruments Cutting machines Joining methods	micrometers lathes soldering, screw-fastening, etc.
12	40	Industrial processes Steam engines Petrol engines	diecasting piston and crank 4-stroke cycle
13	45	Electromagnetism Materials Measuring instruments	conductors metals electrical meters
14	48	Fault-finding Measuring instruments Electrical components	electrical ignition dials generators, transformers

Unit	Page	Topic	Example
15	53	Materials Joining methods	plastics, metals thermal, mechanical and adhesive
16	57	Electrical connections Personal safety Materials protection	multicore wire, batteries corrosion, marking, etc.
17	62	Joining methods Materials	riveting metal properties
18	65	Structural safety Joining methods	beams, girders brazing, welding, etc.
19	69	Industrial processes Electronic components	furnaces rectifiers
20	73	Personal safety Fault-finding Industrial processes	 riveting machining, casting and forging
21	77	Thermostatic controls	bimetal strip, hot-water thermostat electric iron
22	80	Refrigeration Petrol engines	compression refrigerator, refrigerants combustion process
23	83	Industrial processes Fault-finding	metal hardening metal hardening, drill damage
24	87	Fault-finding	fuel consumption, ignition, electrics

Unit 1

Presentation

1 one 2 two 3 three 4 four
5 five 6 six

Read the text and label Figure 1.1:

Triangles are shapes; they have three sides.
Hexagons are shapes; they have six sides.
Squares and rectangles have four sides.
Circles do not have sides.

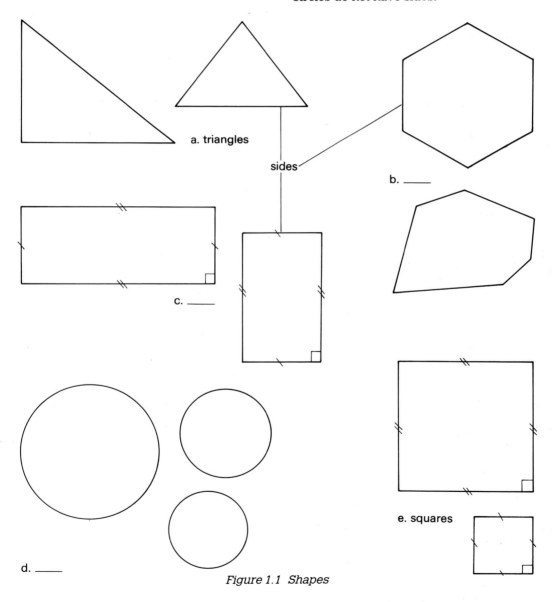

Figure 1.1 Shapes

1

Unit 1

Practice

Look at Figure 1.2 and complete the text:

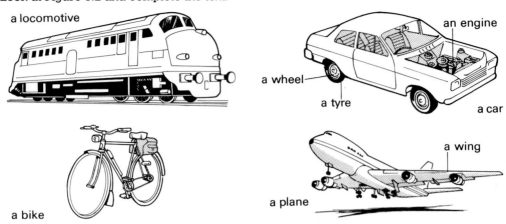

Figure 1.2

Bikes, planes and cars ____ wheels and tyres. ____ have wheels; they do not ____ tyres. Bikes ____ two wheels and two tyres. ____have wings. Bikes, locomotives and cars ____ ____ ____ wings. ____, ____ and ____ have engines. ____ do not have engines.

Development 1

Look at Table 1.1 and complete the sentences:

	wheels	tyres	engines	wings
cars	✓ (YES)	✓ (YES)	✓ (YES)	✗ (NO)
locomotives	✓	✗	✓	✗
planes	✓	✓	✓	✓
bikes	✓	✓	✗	✗

Table 1.1

For example:

1 Cars have wheels and tyres; bikes *also* have wheels and tyres.
2 Planes have wings *but* bikes, cars and locomotives do not (have wings).

1 Cars have wheels and tyres; bikes ____ have wheels and tyres.
2 Planes have wings ____ bikes, cars and locomotives do not.

3 Cars, locomotives and planes have engines ____ bikes do not.
4 Cars have wheels and tyres; bikes ____ have wheels and tyres.
5 Locomotives have wheels ____ they do not have tyres.
6 Planes have wheels; they ____ have tyres.

Development 2

Join the sentences and parts of sentences in the right order:

Start:
Squares and rectangles are shapes.
Squares have four sides. ____ .

a. Rectangles also have four sides.
b. .. they have three sides.
c. Circles are also shapes ..
d. **Squares have four sides.**
e. .. they do not have sides.
f. .. but ..
g. Triangles do not; ..
h. **Squares and rectangles are shapes.**

Summary

Sentence Patterns

Squares and rectangles **are** shapes.
Triangles **have** three sides.
Bikes **have** two wheels and two tyres.

Connectors

Addition

A + B

Squares **and** rectangles have four sides.
Cars have wheels **and** tyres.

Exception

$A_1(\checkmark); A_2(\times)$

Circles are shapes **but** they do not have sides.
Locomotives have wheels **but** they do not have tyres.

Similarity

A = C; B = C

Squares have four sides; rectangles **also** have four sides.

Reference

Locomotives have wheels but **they** do not have tyres.
Squares are shapes; **they** have four sides.

Selected Vocabulary

shapes:
  triangles
  squares
  rectangles
  hexagons
  circles

forms of transport:
  bikes
  planes
  cars
  locomotives

components:
  wheels
  tyres
  wings
  engines
  sides

Unit 2

Presentation

---

7 seven 8 eight 9 nine 10 ten
11 eleven 12 twelve

Read the text and label Figure 2.1:

Cars have an engine and a gearbox. Some
cars have a petrol engine and some cars
have a diesel engine. Some cars have a
manual gearbox and some have an
automatic gearbox. Most cars ($> 50\%$)
have a petrol engine; most also have a
manual gearbox. Cars also have a
generator: some have a dynamo and
some have an alternator.

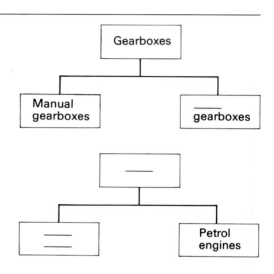

Figure 2.1

Practice

Choose a, b or c etc; for example:

   a. Cars | have a diesel engine.
   b. Most cars |
   c. *Some cars* |

1 a. Triangles | have three sides.
  b. Some triangles |
  c. Most triangles |

2 a. Most locomotives | have twelve wheels.
  b. Locomotives |
  c. Some locomotives |

3 a. Some cars | have four wheels but | d. cars | have three wheels.
  b. Most cars | | e. some cars |
  c. Cars | | f. most cars |

4 a. Shapes | have eight sides.
  b. Some shapes |
  c. Most shapes |

5 a. Most cars | do not have a diesel engine.
  b. Some cars |
  c. Cars |

Unit 2

Development

Choose a, b or c etc. to complete the text:

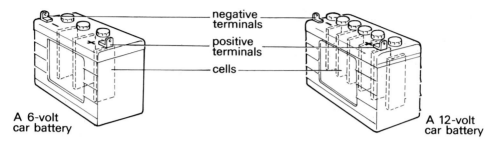

Figure 2.2 Car batteries

a. Cars	have a battery.	d. Cars	have a 12-volt battery,
b. Some cars		e. Some cars	
c. Most cars		f. Most cars	

but	g. cars	have a 6-volt battery.	j. 12-volt car batteries
	h. some cars		k. Some 12-volt car batteries
	i. most cars		l. Most 12-volt car batteries

have six cells, but	m. 6-volt car batteries	have three cells.
	n. some 6-volt car batteries	
	o. most 6-volt car batteries	

p. Car batteries	have positive and negative terminals.
q. Some car batteries	
r. Most car batteries	

Summary

Sentence Patterns

12-volt car batteries **have** six cells.
Most cars **have** a manual gearbox.
Some car batteries **have** three cells.

Reference

Most cars have a petrol engine; **most**
also have a manual gearbox.
Cars have a generator: **some** have a
dynamo and **some** have an alternator.

Selected Vocabulary

car components:

petrol engines
diesel engines

manual gearboxes
automatic gearboxes

12-volt batteries
6-volt batteries

generators (dynamos
and alternators)

battery components:

positive terminals
negative terminals
cells

Unit 3

Presentation

Read the text and complete Table 3.1:

Aluminium (Al), water (H_2O), oxygen (O_2) and carbon dioxide (CO_2) are substances. Some substances are elements and some substances are compounds. Elements have only one type of atom whereas compounds have more than one type.

Aluminium is an element: it has only one type of atom (i.e. it has only aluminium atoms). Oxygen has only one type of atom, so it is also an element.

Carbon dioxide has two types of atom (carbon and oxygen), so it is a compound. Sulphuric acid (H_2SO_4) is also a compound: it has three types of atom (hydrogen, sulphur and oxygen). Water is also a compound.

Substances	
_____	compounds
aluminium	____
_____	sulphuric acid
hydrogen	____
etc.	etc.

Table 3.1

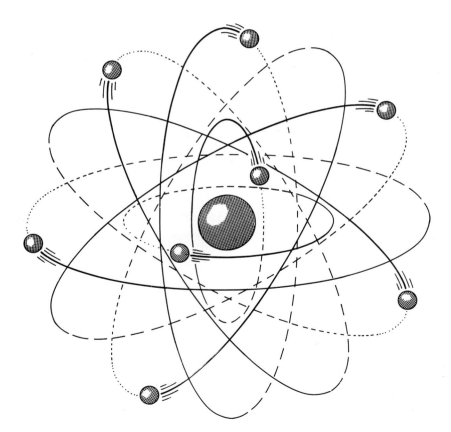

Figure 3.1 Model of an atom

Practice 1

Complete the sentences. For example:

1 Aluminium has only one type of atom, so it is <u>an element.</u>
2 Hydrogen has only one type of atom, so it is an element.

---

1 Aluminium has only one type of atom, so it is ____ ____ .

2 Hydrogen has only one type of atom, so ____ .
3 Water has more than one type of atom, so ____ ____ a compound.
4 Carbon dioxide ____ .
5 Iron (Fe) ____ .
6 Salt (NaCl) ____ .
7 Copper (Cu) ____ .

Practice 2

Use Figure 3.2 to complete the sentences:

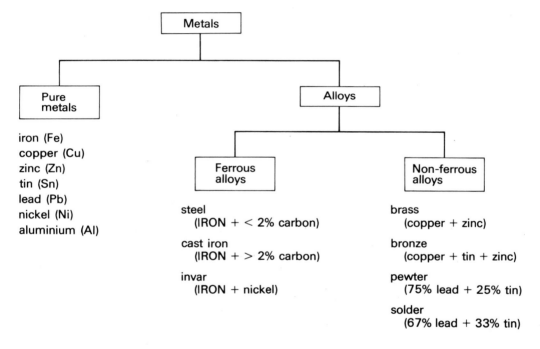

Figure 3.2 Types of metal

For example:

1 Brass is an alloy *whereas* aluminium *is a pure metal.*
2 Brass and pewter *are non-ferrous alloys* whereas steel is *a ferrous alloy.*

---

1 Brass is an alloy ____ aluminium ____ .
2 Brass and pewter ____ whereas steel is ____ .

3 Brass and bronze ____ copper alloys ____ and ____ lead alloys.
4 Zinc ____ an element ____ pewter ____ .
5 Solder ____ whereas invar ____ .
6 Steel has less than 2% of carbon ____ cast iron ____ .

Development

Use Figure 3.3 to connect the sentences in the correct order:

Start:
Pure metals are chemical elements but most industrial metals are alloys. ____

a. Steel and invar are examples of ferrous alloys ..
b. **Pure metals are chemical elements** ..
c. Bronze is also a non-ferrous alloy.
d. Some alloys are ferrous and some are non-ferrous.
e. .. whereas brass is non-ferrous.
f. .. whereas non-ferrous alloys do not have iron.
g. .. **but most industrial metals are alloys.**
h. In ferrous alloys, iron is one of the substances ..

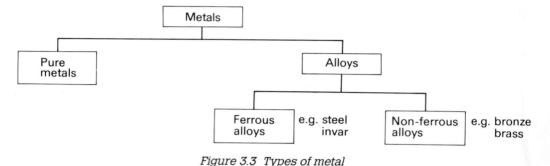

Figure 3.3 Types of metal

Summary

Sentence Patterns

Aluminium **is** an element.
Bronze and brass **are** non-ferrous alloys.

Aluminium **has** one type of atom.
Pure metals **have** one type of atom.

Connectors

Difference

$A \neq B$ Elements have only one type of atom **whereas** compounds have more than one type.

Deduction

$A \therefore B$ Iron is one of the substances in steel, **so** steel is a ferrous alloy.

Explanation

$A = B$ Copper and zinc are pure metals: they have only one type of atom.

Copper and zinc are pure metals; **i.e.** they have only one type of atom.

Reference

Oxygen has only one type of atom, so **it** is an element.
Aluminium is a pure metal: **it** has only aluminium atoms.
Oxygen and hydrogen are elements, so **they** only have one type of atom.

Selected Vocabulary

substances:

chemical elements (see Table 3.1)
chemical compounds (see Table 3.1)

types of metal (see Figure 3.2):

pure metals
alloys (industrial metals)

Unit 4

Presentation

Complete the text and Figure 4.1:

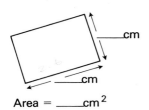

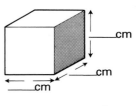

_____cm

_____cm

_____cm

_____cm

_____cm

_____cm

_____cm

Area = _____cm ^{2} Area = _____cm ^{2} Volume = _____cm ^{3}

Figure 4.1

In Fig. 4.1 there are three shapes: a rectangle, a circle and a cube. The rectangle has a length and a width: the length is 2.6 cm and the width is 1.7 cm. Therefore, the area is 4.42 cm².

The circle has a radius (r), a diameter (D) and a circumference (C): the radius is 1 cm, the diameter is 2 cm and the circumference is approximately 6.28 cm, so the area is approximately 3.14 cm².

Therefore, if the radius of a circle is 2 cm, the area is approximately 12.6 cm² (Area = πr²).

The cube has a length, a width and a height: the height, the length and the width are all 2 cm, so the volume is _____ cm³. Therefore, if the length, width and height of a cube are all 5 cm, the volume is _____ cm³.

Practice 1

Look at Figures 4.1, 4.2 and 4.3 and complete the statements:

For example:

1 *The area of **a** rectangle*
   = length × width
2 *The area of **the** rectangle in Figure 4.1*
   = 4.42 cm².

1 ____ = length × width
2 ____ = 4.42 cm²

3 ____ = πD
4 ____ = $\dfrac{b \times h}{2}$
5 ____ = πr²h
6 ____ = 5 cm²
7 ____ = 8 cm³
8 ____ = 3.14 cm² (approx.)
9 ____ = 4.71 cm³ (approx.)
10 ____ = 2.6 cm

h = 2 cm
b = 5 cm

h

b

Figure 4.2 A triangle

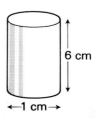

6 cm

←1 cm→

Figure 4.3 A cylinder

Practice 2

Complete the sentences:

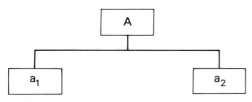

For example:

1 *There are two main types of metal:*
pure metals and alloys.

1 ____: pure metals and alloys.
2 There are two main types of car
generator: ____.
3 There are two main types of
substance: ____.
4 ____: ferrous and non-ferrous.
5 There are two main types of car
engine: ____.
6 ____: 6-volt and 12-volt.

Practice 3

Use Figures 4.4 and 4.5 to complete the
sentences:

For example:

1 If the movement of the bottom pulley is
anticlockwise, the movement of the *top
pulley* is also *anticlockwise*.

1 If the movement of the bottom pulley is
anticlockwise, the movement of the ____
is also ____.
2 If ____ is clockwise, the movement of
the bottom pulley ____.
3 ____ front sprocket is anticlockwise,
____.
4 ____ small gear ____, ____.

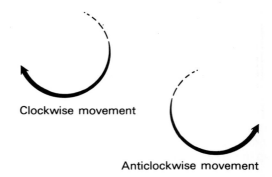

Clockwise movement

Anticlockwise movement

Figure 4.4 Rotary movement

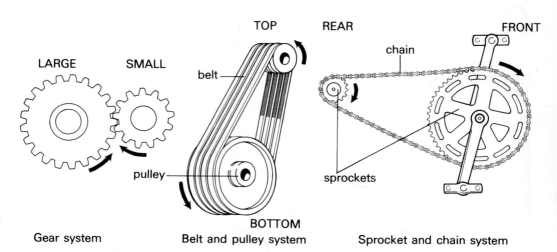

Gear system

Belt and pulley system

Sprocket and chain system

Figure 4.5 Types of rotary drive

Development

Read the text on the left; then complete the text on the right:

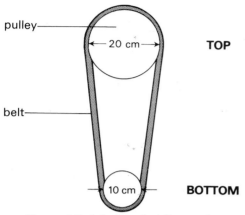

Figure 4.6 A belt and pulley system

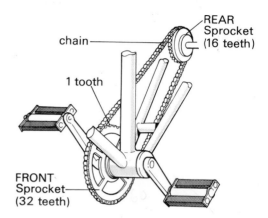

Figure 4.7 A sprocket and chain system

In pulley systems, the diameter of the pulleys is very important. In the pulley system in Figure 4.6, the diameter of the top pulley is 20 cm and the diameter of the bottom pulley is 10 cm.

If the speed of the top pulley is 100 revolutions per minute (100 rev/min), the speed of the bottom pulley is 200 rev/min.

Therefore:

speed of bottom pulley = speed of top pulley × $\dfrac{\text{diameter of top pulley}}{\text{diameter of bottom pulley}}$

Bikes have a sprocket and chain system. The number of teeth on the sprockets is very important. On the bike in Figure 4.7, the ____ ____ has 32 teeth and ____.

If ____ front sprocket is 60 rev/min, the ____.

Therefore:

____

Summary

Sentence Patterns

In Figure 4.1 **there are** 3 shapes.
There are 3 shapes *in Figure 4.1*.
There are two main types of substances.
The area of a rectangle = length × width.
The area of the rectangle in Figure 4.1 **is** 4.42 cm².

Connectors

Deduction

A ∴ B   The height, length and width of the cube in Figure 4.1 are 2 cm; **therefore** the volume is 8 cm³.

Hypothesis

A ∴ B   **If** the length, width and height of a cube are 5 cm, the volume is 125 cm³.

Unit 4

Reference

The cube in Figure 4.1 has a ⎡length⎤, a ⎡width⎤ and a ⎡height⎤; **the** ⎡length⎤, **the** ⎡width⎤ and **the** ⎡height⎤ are all 2 cm.

There are 3 ⎡shapes in Figure 4.1⎤: **the** ⎡rectangle⎤ has an area of 4.42 cm², **the** ⎡circle⎤ has an area of 3.142 cm² and **the** ⎡cube⎤ has a volume of 125 cm³.

⎡Circles⎤ have a ⎡diameter⎤, a ⎡radius⎤ and a ⎡circumference⎤; **the** ⎡diameter⎤ of **the** ⎡circle⎤ in Figure 4.1 is 2 cm, **the** ⎡radius⎤ is 1 cm and **the** ⎡circumference⎤ is 6.28 cm.

Selected Vocabulary

rotary system components:

1. belts
2. pulleys
3. gears
4. sprockets
5. chains

6. shapes:
7. cubes
8. cylinders

9. dimensions and measurements:
10. length   11. radius
12. height   13. diameter
14. width   circumference
15. volume
16. area   17. speed

rotary movement:
    clockwise movement
18. anticlockwise movement

12

Unit 5

Presentation

Use Fig. 5.1 to complete the text:

To find the area of ABCDEF,

either:
1 Calculate the area of AGEF. (Multiply AG by AF.)
2 Calculate ____ GBCD. (Multiply GB ____ GD.)
3 Add AGEF to ____.

or:
1 Find the area of ABHF. (____.)
2 ____ CDEH. (____.)
3 Subtract ____ from ____.

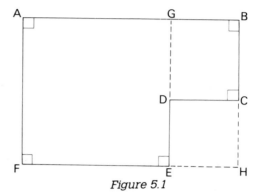

Figure 5.1

Practice
Use Fig. 5.2 to complete the sentences:

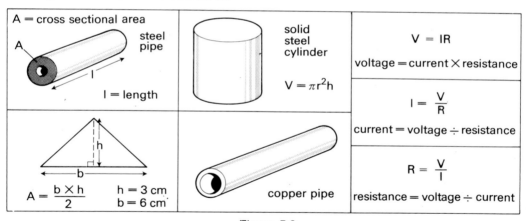

Figure 5.2

For example:
1 *To find the volume of steel in the pipe, multiply the cross-sectional area by the length.*
2 To find the resistance in an electrical circuit, *divide the voltage by the current.*

1 ____, multiply the cross-sectional area by the length.

2 To find the resistance in an electrical circuit, ____.
3 ____, multiply the current by the resistance.
4 ____, use the formula $v = \pi r^2 h$.
5 To find the volume of copper in the pipe, ____.
6 To find the area of the triangle, ____.
7 To find the current in an electrical circuit, ____.

13

Development

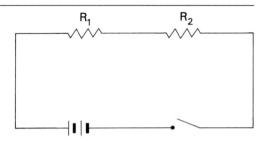

1st 2nd 3rd 4th 5th 6th
first second third fourth fifth sixth

Read the text; use Figs. 5.3, 5.4 and 5.5 to do the calculations:

The electric circuit in Fig. 5.3 has two resistors in series: the first resistor has a value of 8 ohms (8 Ω) and the second has a value of 12 Ω. To find the resistance in the circuit, add the value of the first resistor to the value of the second resistor:

$$R = R_1 + R_2$$

Therefore

$$R = \underline{\hphantom{--}} + \underline{\hphantom{--}} = \underline{\hphantom{--}} \; \Omega$$

Figure 5.3 Resistors in series

In the circuit in Fig. 5.4 there are three resistors in parallel: the first one has a value of 12 Ω, the second one has a value of 8 Ω and the value of the third one is also 8 Ω. To find the total resistance in the circuit, use the formula

$$\frac{1}{R} = \frac{1}{R_1} + \frac{1}{R_2} + \frac{1}{R_3}$$

Therefore

$$\frac{1}{R} = \underline{\hphantom{----}} = \underline{\hphantom{--}} \; \Omega$$

$$\therefore \; R = \underline{\hphantom{--}} \; \Omega$$

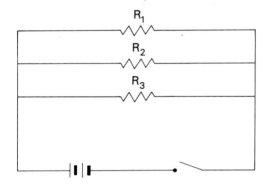

Figure 5.4 Resistors in parallel

The circuit in Fig. 5.5 has a total resistance of 20 Ω. If R_1 has a value of 14 Ω, subtract R_1 from the total resistance to find the value of R_2:

$$R_2 = \underline{\hphantom{----}} = \underline{\hphantom{--}}$$

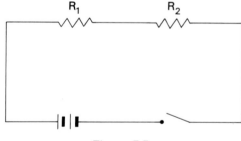

Figure 5.5

Summary

Sentence Patterns

Calculate the area of AGEF.
Find the area of ABHF.
Add the area of AGEF *to the area of GDCB.*
Multiply the current *by the resistance.*
To find the area of a rectangle, **multiply** the length *by the width.*

Connectors

Alternatives
A/B **Either** add AGEF to GBCD **or** subtract DCHE from ABHF.

Reference

ABC: A =   There are ⬚3 resistors in Fig. 5.4:
    B =   the first **one** has a value of 12 Ω,
    C =   the value of the second **one** is
    8 Ω and the third **one** also has a
    value of 8 Ω.

Selected Vocabulary

mathematical operations:

add
subtract
multiply
divide

calculate
find

electrical concepts:

resistance
voltage
current

a circuit

resistors in parallel
resistors in series

dimensions and measurements:

ohms (Ω)
cross-sectional area
a value

Unit 6

Presentation

Read the text and complete Fig. 6.1:

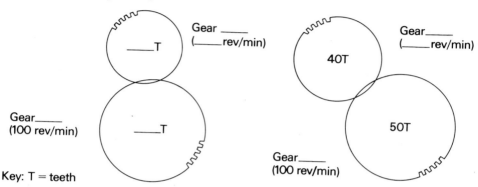

Gear _____
(_____ rev/min)

_____T

Gear_____
(100 rev/min)

_____T

Key: T = teeth

Gear_____
(_____ rev/min)

40T

50T

Gear_____
(100 rev/min)

Figure 6.1

In Fig. 6.1 there are two gear systems. In the system on the left there are two gears: A and B. Gear A has a smaller number of teeth, so it has a faster speed than Gear B. They have 36 and 45 teeth respectively, so the ratio of the number of teeth on A to the number of teeth on B is 4 to 5 (4:5). The gear speed ratio is therefore 5:4 (i.e. it is the opposite of the ratio of gear teeth).

In the system on the right there are also 2 gears: C and D. Gear D has a greater number of teeth, so it has a slower speed. C and D are a different size from A and B but they have the same size ratio of 4:5. They therefore have the same gear speed ratio as A:B. So, if the two faster gears (A and C) have the same speed, the speeds of B and D are also the same.

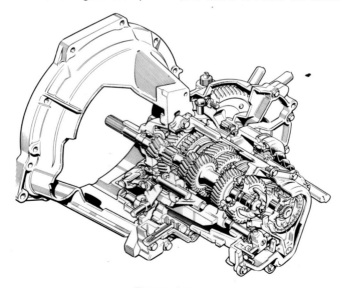

Figure 6.2

16

Unit 6

Practice 1
Use Fig. 6.3 to complete the sentences:

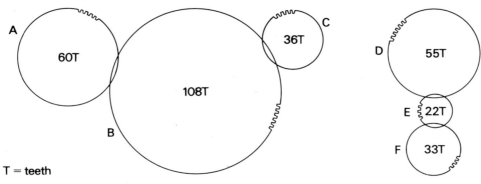

T = teeth

Figure 6.3

For example:

1 D has a *greater* number of teeth *than* F.

1 D has a ——— number of teeth ——— F.
2 B has a ——— diameter ———C.
3 F has a ——— speed ——— ——— .
4 ——— has a faster speed ——— F.

5 The speed of ——— is slower than the speed of ——— .
6 C has a smaller ——— ——— ——— ——— A, so A has a ——— speed.
7 B has a greater number of teeth than A; the speed of ——— is therefore ——— .

Practice 2
Choose a, b, c, d, e to complete the sentences. Use Figs. 6.3 and 6.4.

the opposite of	a	■	is the opposite of	⬤
the same as	b	☐+	is the same as	☐+
the same	c	☐+	and ☐+	are the same
different from	d	☐+	is different from	☐+
different	e	☐+	and ☐+	are different

Figure 6.4

1 The ratio of the number of teeth is ____ the size ratio.
2 The two gear systems in Fig. 6.3 are ____ .
3 A : C and D : F are ____ .

4 The movement of A is ____ the movement of B.
5 The speed of B is ____ the speed of A.
6 The direction of movement of D is ____ the direction of movement of F.

Practice 3

Complete Table 6.1:

The ZX 1000 electric drill has two speeds: the fast speed is 3,000 rpm and the slower speed is 1,000 rpm. Adjust the speed according to the type of material and the size of the hole. For example, use the faster speed for a soft material such as wood to drill holes smaller than 10 millimetres (10 mm) in diameter but choose the slower speed for holes between 10 and 25 mm. However, for steel, a hard material, use the faster speed for holes smaller than 6.5 mm and choose the slower speed to drill holes between 6.5 and 10 mm.

Figure 6.5

Speed	Material	Diameter	
1, 000 rev/min			< = smaller than
			> = greater than
		10 mm – 25 mm	
		< 6·5 mm	

Table 6.1

Practice 4

Use Fig. 6.6 and the words in the box to complete the text:

| greatest | softest | quickest |
| smallest | *hardest* | slowest |

Hard steel is the *hardest* material in the table. Drills for hard steel have the _____ point angle and the _____ helix angle. They have the _____ spiral.

Aluminium is the _____ material in the table. Drills for aluminium have the _____ helix angle and the _____ point angle. They have the _____ spiral.

	Helix angle	Type of spiral	Point angle
For hard steel	5° to 10°	slow	130°
For mild steel	25°	standard	118°
For aluminium	40°	quick	90°

Figure 6.6 Types of drill for different metals

Development

Read the text to find speeds A and E and to find apertures U and Z:

The SLR 21 has 5 shutter speeds. The fastest shutter speed is $\frac{1}{500}$ of a second and the slowest is $\frac{1}{30}$ sec. To select the higher speeds, turn the shutter speed control anticlockwise; for the lower speeds, turn it clockwise.

The camera has 6 aperture settings between f16 and f2. The smaller the f number, the larger the diameter of the aperture; the largest aperture is therefore f2. To increase the aperture (i.e. to choose the larger apertures), turn the aperture control *clockwise* (from the front of the camera); to decrease the aperture, turn the control anticlockwise.

Speeds:
  A = _____
  E = _____
Apertures:
  U = _____
  Z = _____

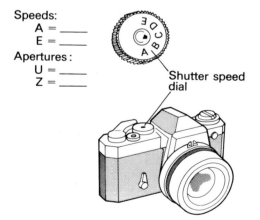

Shutter speed dial

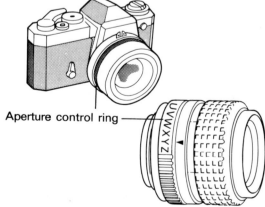

Aperture control ring

Figure 6.7 SLR 21 camera

Unit 6

Summary

Sentence Patterns

Turn the shutter speed control *anticlockwise for the higher speed.*
For larger holes, **choose** the slower speed.

Choose the slower speed *to drill holes between 6.5 and 10 mm.*

To decrease the aperture, **turn** the control *anticlockwise.*

Connectors

Difference

A ≠ B   For wood, choose the slower speed for holes between 10 and 25 mm; **however**, for steel, use the slower speed to drill holes between 6.5 mm and 10 mm.

Reference

ABC: A, B, C   Gears D, E and F   have   55 , 22 and 33 teeth **respectively**.

Selected Vocabulary

operating instructions:

choose	increase
select	decrease
use	turn
adjust	

properties:

hard
soft
mild

size:

small
great

speed:

slow	low
fast	high

Unit 7

Presentation

Read the text and label Figs. 7.1 and 7.2:

There are different types of chisel for metalwork and for woodwork. Woodwork chisels have a smaller angle at the point of the tool. Although this is suitable for soft materials such as wood, a tool point with a small angle is too weak for hard materials. To cut metal, a stronger point is necessary, so the angle is greater at the point of a metalwork chisel.

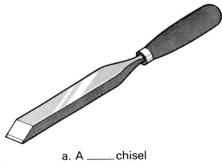

a. A ____ chisel

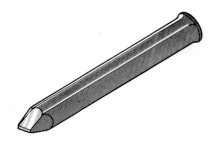

b. A ____ chisel

Figure 7.1

There are several important angles at the point of a metalwork chisel:

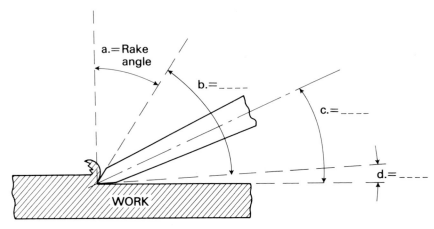

Figure 7.2 Metalwork chisel tool point

The angle between the lower surface of the tool point and the work surface is called the clearance angle.

The angle between the upper surface of the tool point and a line perpendicular (i.e. at 90°) to the work is known as the rake angle.

The cutting angle is the angle between the upper and lower surfaces of the tool point.

The angle between the centre of the chisel shank and the work surface is termed the angle of inclination.

Practice 1

Use Fig. 7.3 to complete the sentences and the key:

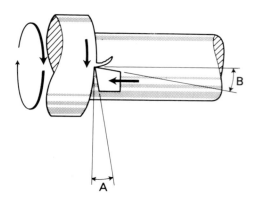

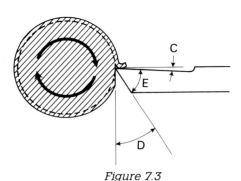

Figure 7.3

Key:
A = Side clearance angle
B = Side _____angle
C = Back rake angle
D = Front _____ _____
E = Wedge angle

Lathe tools have two clearance angles and two rake angles:
Angle A is called _____.
Angle B _____.
_____ is known as _____.
_____ front _____.
_____ is termed _____.

Figure 7.4 A lathe

Practice 2

Read the text and complete the key to Fig. 7.5:

There are two types of rake. In the diagram below, the type of rake on the tool with the weaker point is called a positive rake. The other tool has a greater wedge angle and is therefore stronger. This type is known as a negative rake.

Key:
A = _____ rake
B = _____ rake

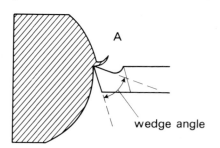

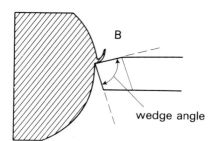

Figure 7.5 Types of rake

Practice 3

Use Fig. 7.6 to complete the sentences about the car engine and transmission system. Use *below*, *above* or *between*. For example:

1 The rocker box is *above* the cylinder head.

1 The rocker box is _____ the cylinder head.

2 The cylinder block is _____ the cylinder head.
3 The sump is _____ the cylinder block.
4 The cylinder block is _____ the sump.
5 The prop shaft is _____ the gearbox and the differential.
6 The differential is _____ the two half shafts.

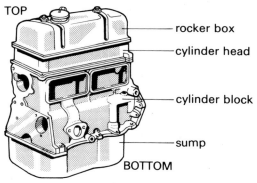
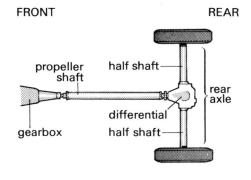

TOP

rocker box
cylinder head
cylinder block
sump

BOTTOM

FRONT   REAR

propeller shaft   half shaft
gearbox   differential   half shaft
rear axle

Figure 7.6 Car power unit and transmission system

Development

Use the text to label the milling machine in Fig. 7.7:

There are two main assemblies at the front of the milling machine above. The upper assembly is called the overarm assembly and the lower one is known as the knee assembly. The latter has three main parts: the knee is at the bottom of the assembly on a vertical column, the top part of the knee assembly is called the work table and the part between the work table and the knee is called the saddle.

The upper assembly also has three main parts: the cutter, the arbor and the overarm. The overarm is the top part of the overarm assembly. The cutter is on a shaft below the overarm and between the two vertical arms. The shaft is called the arbor. The work table is below the cutter.

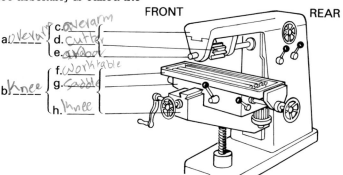

FRONT   REAR

a. overarm
   c. overarm
   d. cutter
   e. arbor
b. knee
   f. worktable
   g. saddle
   h. knee

Figure 7.7 Knee-type horizontal milling-machine

Summary

Sentence Patterns

Angle A **is called** the side clearance angle.

The lower assembly **is known as** the knee assembly.

The angle between the centre of the chisel shank and the work surface **is termed** the angle of inclination.

Connectors

Restriction

A (✓); B (×) **Although** a small angle is suitable for soft materials, it is too weak for hard materials.

Reference

In the diagram **below**, the type of rake on the tool with the weaker point is called a positive rake. (See Practice 2)

There are two main assemblies at the front of the milling machine **above**. (See Development)

Selected Vocabulary

positions and places:

(the) lower (surface)
(the) upper (assembly)

the top	above (the saddle)
the centre	between (the gearbox and differential)
the bottom	below (the overarm)

the front
the rear/the back
the side

tools and machines:

a woodwork chisel	a lathe
a metalwork chisel	a milling machine
a lathe tool	

cutting tool terminology: (See Fig. 7.3 Key)

car components: (See Fig. 7.6)

milling machine components: (See Fig. 7.7)

machine and tool components:

a shaft	a cutter
an arm	a tool-point/a point
an assembly	

Unit 8

Presentation

Select the correct instructions for the actions in Fig. 8.1:

For example:

A = 2

1 Turn the jack handle anticlockwise to lower the car.

2 Turn the gear wheel anticlockwise to raise the drill.
3 Turn the bolt clockwise to tighten it.
4 Press the top button to stop the motor.
5 Press the largest pedal to stop the car.
6 Pull the handle down to cut the metal bar.
7 Push the bar down to raise the load.

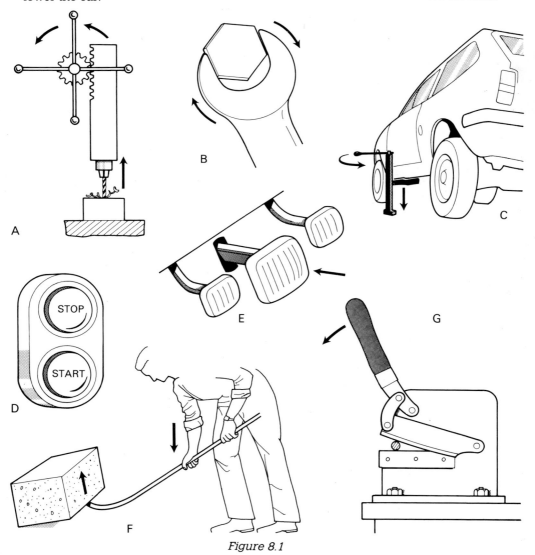

Figure 8.1

Practice 1

Use the diagrams below and words in the Presentation to complete the instructions:

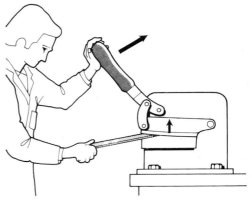

4 _____ the handle up to raise the blade.

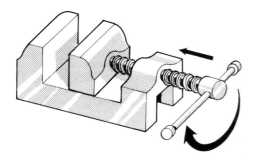

1 _____ the handle clockwise to close the vice jaws.

5 _____ the dial clockwise to decrease the speed.

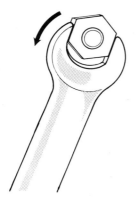

2 _____ the bolt anticlockwise to slacken it.

6 _____ the dial anticlockwise to increase the temperature.

3 _____ the handle up to open the door.

7 _____ the bottom button _____.

Practice 2

Read the instructions for the dynamo belt on the left; then complete the instructions for the alternator belt on the right:

OUP 850 saloon cars have two types of generator: dynamos and alternators.

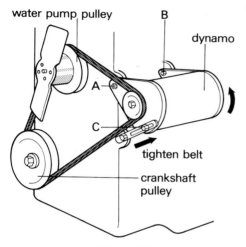

Figure 8.2

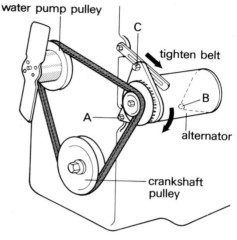

Figure 8.3

Fan belt adjustment on models with a dynamo.

1 Slacken mounting bolts A and B.
2 Slacken the slide bolt C.
3 Either: a. pull the dynamo up to tighten the belt
      or: b. push the dynamo down to slacken the belt.
4 Tighten the slide bolt.
5 Tighten the mounting bolts.

Fan belt adjustment on models with an alternator.

1 _ _ _ _.
2 _ _ _ _.
3 Either: a. _ _ _ _.
      or: b. _ _ _ _.
4 _ _ _ _.
5 _ _ _ _.

Development

Read the text, label Fig. 8.4 and solve the problem:

In a petrol engine, the movement of the pistons between the bottom and top of the cylinder is termed the piston stroke. The highest position of the piston is called the Top Dead Centre (TDC) position (see Fig. 8.4). When the piston is in this position, the volume between the cylinder head and the top of the piston is known as the clearance volume.

The lowest position of the piston is called the Bottom Dead Centre (BDC) position. The difference between the clearance volume and the total volume when the piston is in the BDC position is called the working volume. In other words, to find the working volume, multiply the length of the piston stroke by the cross-sectional area of the cylinder.

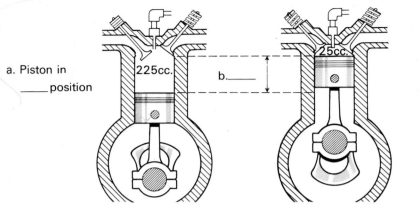

a. Piston in _____ position

b._____

c. Piston in _____ position

225cc.

25cc.

Figure 8.4

To find the compression ratio of an engine, divide the total volume when the piston is in the BDC position (i.e. the working volume + clearance volume) by the clearance volume. Therefore, for the engine in Fig. 8.4:

$$(\_\_\_\_ + \_\_\_\_) \div \_\_\_\_ = \_\_\_\_.$$

The engine therefore has a _____ : _____ compression ratio.

Summary

Sentence Patterns

Turn the jack handle *anticlockwise to lower the car.*

When the piston is in the BDC position, the difference between the clearance volume and the total volume **is called** the working volume.

The difference between the clearance volume and the total volume *when the piston is in the BDC position* **is called** the working volume.

Selected Vocabulary

operating instructions:

open	close
pull	push
lower	raise
tighten	slacken
press	

petrol engine terminology:

piston stroke
compression ratio
clearance volume

other useful words:

a bolt	a dial
a button	a door
a pedal	a vice
a bar	a handle
a blade	

Unit 9

Presentation

Use Figs. 9.1 and 9.2 to complete the text:

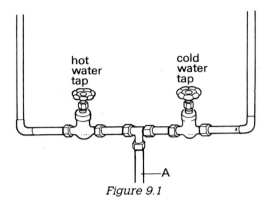

Figure 9.1

The two taps in Fig. 9.1 **control** the water flow. They also **control** the temperature of the water at point A.

The tap _ _ _ _ **controls** the hot water flow; the tap _ _ _ _ **controls** the cold water flow.

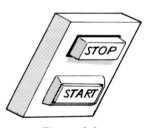

Figure 9.2

Fig. 9.2 **shows** a stop/start switch. The two buttons **control** an electric motor. The _ _ _ _ **starts** the motor; the _ _ _ _ stops it.

Practice 1

Now use the words in the box to describe the function of the lift buttons in Fig. 9.3:

| closes opens stops |
| stop   shows has |

Fig. 9.3 _____ the control panel for a lift. Each button _____ a different function. The one at the top on the left _____ the lift doors; the one at the bottom on the left _____ them. The one in the middle on the left _____ the lift. The ones on the right _____ the lift at the different floors.

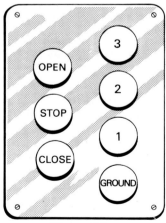

Figure 9.3

29

Practice 2
Read the text and complete the key to Fig. 9.4:

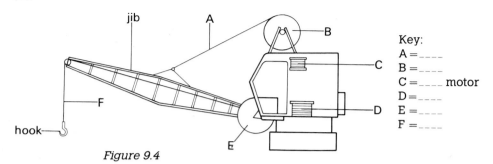

jib   A   B   C   D   F   hook   E

Key:
A = ____
B = ____
C = ____ motor
D = ____
E = ____
F = ____

Figure 9.4

The diagram above shows a crane; this has two motors. The motors turn the drums to raise or lower the jib or the hook. The top drum controls the movement of the jib cable, i.e. it raises and lowers the jib. The other drum controls the movement of the hook cable to raise or lower the hook.

Practice 3
Complete the sentences:

1 The ____ cable raises and lowers the jib.
2 The ____ ____ raises and lowers the hook.
3 The ____ cable drum controls the movement of the jib cable.
4 The ____ ____ ____ controls the movement of the hook cable.
5 The ____ ____ ____ motor turns the jib cable drum.
6 The ____ drum.

Practice 4
Use Fig. 9.5 to join the sentences and parts of sentences in the correct order:

Start:

The rotary movement of the crankshaft turns the crankshaft pulley to drive the fan belt. ____

a. .. to cool the water in the engine.
b. .. **to drive the fan belt**.
c. .. **turns the crankshaft pulley** ..
d. .. turns the dynamo ..
e. .. the fan pulley ..
f. **The rotary movement of the crankshaft** ..
g. This turns the two smaller pulleys.
h. .. drives the water pump and the fan ..
i. The smallest pulley ..
j. .. to generate electricity; ..

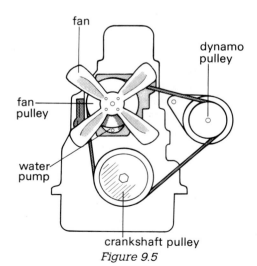

fan   dynamo pulley   fan pulley   water pump   crankshaft pulley

Figure 9.5

Development

Use the description of the cooling system to complete the description of the lubricating system; refer to Figs. 9.6 and 9.7:

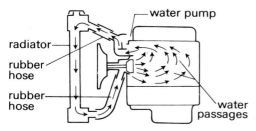

Figure 9.6 Cooling system

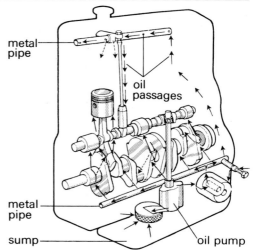

Figure 9.7 Lubricating system

Most cars use water to cool the engine. Water flows from the radiator through a system of water passages and rubber hoses. A water pump pushes the water round. This system is known as the cooling system.

Cars use _____ to lubricate the _____.
Oil _ _ _ _

Summary

Sentence Patterns

The tap *on the left* **controls** the hot water flow.
The fan belt **turns** the two smaller pulleys.

The two buttons **control** an electric motor.
The crane motors **turn** the pulleys.

The other pulley **controls** the movement of the hook cable *to raise or lower the hook.*
The motors **turn** the pulleys *to raise or lower the jib or the hook.*

Reference

The diagram above shows a crane ; **this** has two motors.
Water flows through a system of water passages and rubber hoses . **This system** is known as the cooling system.
The crane has two pulleys: **one** controls the jib cable, **the other** controls the hook cable.

Selected Vocabulary

functions and processes:

control	lubricate
start	flow
stop	drive
show	generate
cool	

engine components:

a crankshaft	a cooling system
a water pump	a lubricating system
an oil pump	
a radiator	
a fan	

other useful words:

an electric motor	a cable
a control panel	a tap
a (stop/start) switch	temperature
a hook	

Unit 10

Presentation

Read the text and label Fig. 10.1:

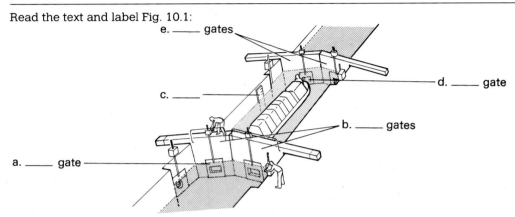

e. _____ gates

d. _____ gate

c. _____

b. _____ gates

a. _____ gate

Figure 10.1 Canal locks

Boats on a canal go through locks to move up or down from one level to another. The locks have large lock gates to let the boats in and out. They also have smaller sluice gates; these open and close to control the water level. The scale on the side of the lock shows the depth of the water in metres.

Practice 1

Use text A to complete text B:

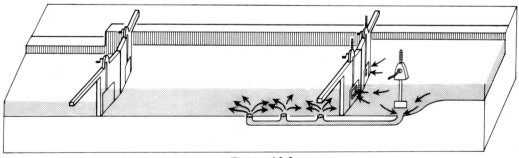

Figure 10.2

A: The upper sluice gates open and let the water in. All the lower gates stay closed while the water level goes up. The upper lock gates do not open until the water level in the lock is the same as the upper level. (Fig. 10.2)

Unit 10

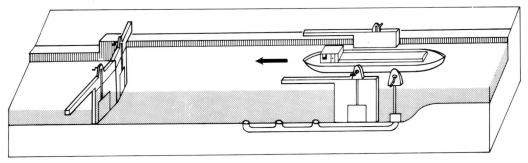

Figure 10.3

When the two levels are the same, the
upper lock gates open and the boat
goes in. Then all the upper gates close.
(Fig. 10.3)

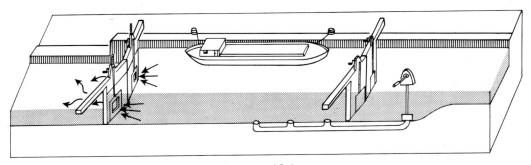

Figure 10.4

B: The lower sluice gates ____. All the
upper gates ____ while ____. The lower
lock gates ____ until ____ (____)

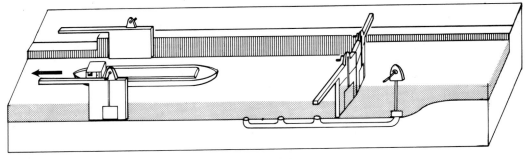

Figure 10.5

When the two levels ____, the lower
lock gates ____ and the boat ____. Then,
all the ____. (____)

Practice 2

Connect the parts of the sentences in the correct order to describe the process in Fig. 10.6:

Start:

When water flows out of the tank the level falls and the ballcock moves down. ____

a. The inward flow of water does not stop ..

b. .. and water flows into the tank.

c. **When water flows out of the tank** ..

d. The downward movement of the ballcock opens the inlet valve ..

e. .. **the level falls and the ballcock moves down.**

f. .. until the ballcock reaches the maximum level and closes the inlet valve.

g. .. the tank water level rises and pushes the ballcock up.

h. When the outward flow of water stops ..

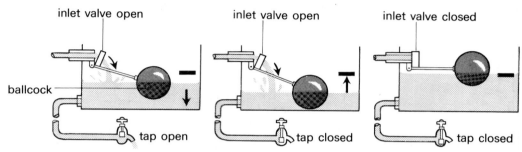

Figure 10.6 Ballcock and valve operation

Development

Read the text and label Fig. 10.7:

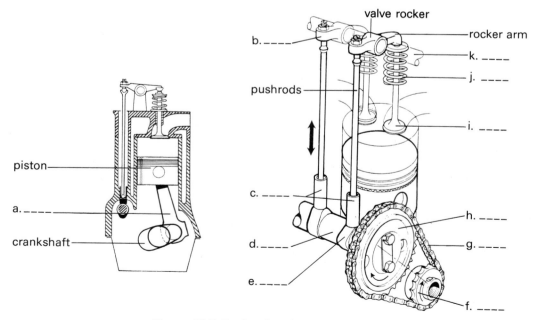

Figure 10.7 Pushrod and valve operation

Unit 10

The two diagrams on p.34 show the pushrod and valve operation in one type of petrol engine.

When the pistons move up and down in the cylinders, the connecting rods push the crankshaft round. This rotary movement also turns the crankshaft sprocket. The crankshaft sprocket drives the timing chain to turn the larger camshaft sprocket. The crankshaft to camshaft speed ratio is 2:1. The camshaft has two cams for each cylinder; there are therefore 8 cams in a 4-cylinder engine, i.e. one for each pushrod.

When the camshaft rotates, the cams raise and lower the cam followers to operate the pushrods. Each cam follower controls one pushrod. When the latter moves up, the top end of the pushrod operates the valve rocker. The rocker shaft does not move, so when the pushrod raises one valve rocker arm, the other arm on the same rocker moves down to open the valve. This downward movement compresses the valve spring. When the cam moves past the highest point, the cam follower and the pushrod fall; the valve spring expands to close the valve.

Summary

Sentence Patterns

The inward flow of water **does not stop**.
The upper lock gates **do not open**.

The inward flow of water **does not stop** *until the ballcock closes the valve.*
The upper lock gates **do not open** *until the lock and upper level are the same.*

The ballcock **moves** *down.*
The boat **goes** *in.*

Water **flows** *out of the tank.*
Water **flows** *into the tank.*

The upper sluice gate **lets** the water *in.*
The connecting rods **push** the crankshaft *round.*

Connectors

Sequence

A→B   **When** the camshaft rotates, the cams raise and lower the cam followers.

A→
B→   All the lower gates stay closed **while** the water level goes up.

A→
→B   The upper lock gates do not open **until** the water level is the same.

Reference

Locks also have $\boxed{\text{smaller sluice gates}}$; **these** open and close to control the water level.

Selected Vocabulary

verbs of motion:

move	rotate
go	compress
reach	expand
rise	fall

movements:

up
down
round
in
out

engine components: (See Fig. 10.7)

other useful words:

a level
a scale
a gate
a valve

Unit 11

Presentation

Read the text and complete Table 11.1:

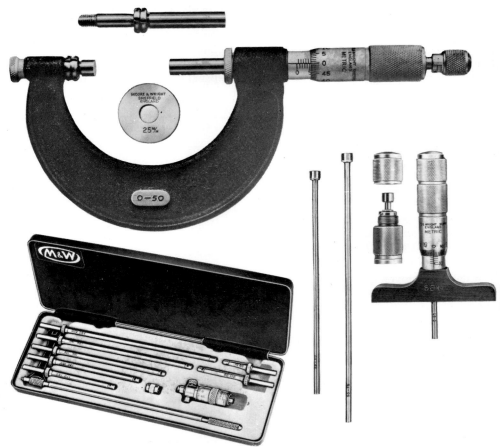

Figure 11.1 Micrometers

To measure dimensions such as the length, height, depth or diameter of a component, micrometers are used. There are different types of micrometer for different dimensions.

To measure the external diameter of a small component such as a small shaft, a micrometer caliper is used; to measure internal diameter, a micrometer cylinder gauge is used. Depth micrometers are used to measure the depth of a component. The measurements are shown on different types of scale depending on the type of micrometer.

micrometer type	dimension
1 micrometer ____	____ diameter
2 ____	____
3 ____	____

Table 11.1

Unit 11

Practice 1

Refer to the diagrams below to complete the sentences:

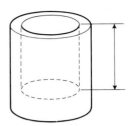

1 To measure the diameter of this ball-bearing, a ____ is used.

2 To measure ____ of this cylinder, a depth micrometer ____.

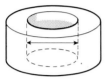

3 ____ the internal ____, a ____.

4 A ____ to ____.

Practice 2

Read the text and solve the problems:

Lathes are used in industry to produce cylindrical items such as shafts or metal cylinders. Two types of movement are used to produce a cylindrical item on a lathe:

1 The rotary movement of the work against the tool-point. The speed of this movement is called the cutting speed. (Fig. 11.2)

2 The linear movement of the tool along the work. This is called the feed, and the speed of this movement is therefore called the feed speed. (Fig. 11.3)

To find the cutting speed, the rotary speed is multiplied by the circumference of the workpiece. Cutting speed is measured in metres per minute (m/min). Therefore, the cutting speed of the tool in Fig. 11.2

$$= \frac{\text{\_\_\_\_} \times \text{\_\_\_\_}}{1000} = \text{\_\_\_\_} \text{ m/min}$$

Feed speeds are measured in millimetres per revolution (mm/rev). To calculate the linear movement of the tool, the feed speed is multiplied by the number of revolutions. Therefore, for the work in Fig. 11.3, the linear movement of the tool in 200 revolutions

$$= \text{\_\_\_\_} \times \text{\_\_\_\_} = \text{\_\_\_\_} \text{ mm.}$$

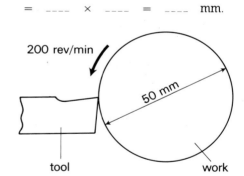

200 rev/min

50 mm

tool

work

Figure 11.2

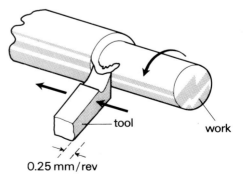

tool

work

0.25 mm/rev

Figure 11.3

37

Development

Use the words in the boxes to complete the text. Refer to the diagrams:

Many different kinds of joint are used to connect pipes together. Three types of fitting for small diameter pipes and three types for pipes with a larger diameter are shown in the diagrams below. However, these are not the only types of pipe joint, and one example of a special fitting is also shown in the bottom diagram.

> are pushed   is pushed   are screwed
> is soldered   is screwed

Small diameter pipes

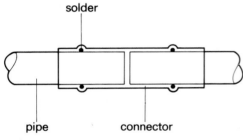

Figure 11.4

a. Each pipe ____ ____ into the connector; the connector ____ ____ to the pipes. (Fig. 11.4)

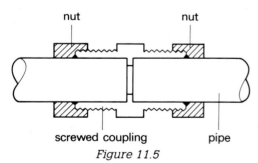

Figure 11.5

b. The pipes ____ ____ into the coupling; then the nuts ____ ____ on. (Fig. 11.5)

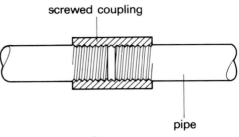

Figure 11.6

c. Each pipe ____ ____ into the threaded coupling. (Fig. 11.6)

> are clamped   are bolted
> are screwed   are welded   are bolted
> are welded   are bolted

Large diameter pipes

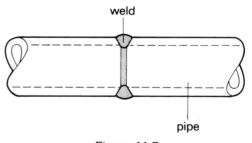

Figure 11.7

d. The ends of the two pipes ____ ____ together. (Fig. 11.7)

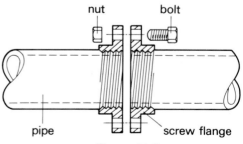

Figure 11.8

e. The flanges ____ ____ onto the pipe. Then they ____ ____ together. (Fig. 11.8)

Unit 11

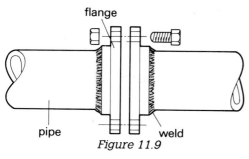

flange

pipe weld

Figure 11.9

f. The flanges _____. Then _____. (Fig. 11.9)

Special fitting

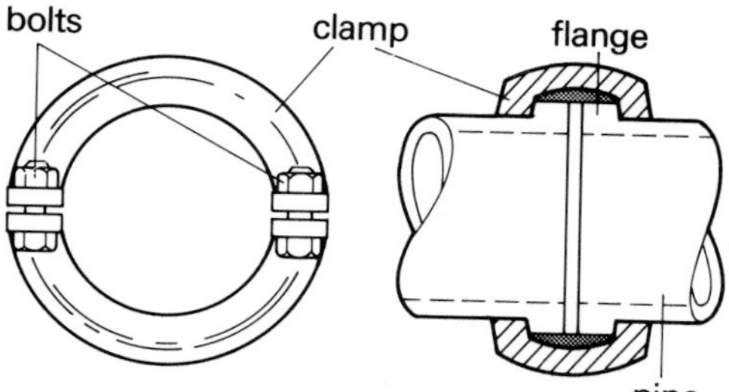

bolts clamp flange

pipe

Figure 11.10

g. The two flanges ____ ____ together.
    Then the clamps ____ ____ together.
    (Fig. 11.10)

Summary

Sentence Patterns

To measure internal diameters, a micrometer cylinder gauge **is used**.

Depth micrometers **are used** *to measure the depth of a component.*

Connectors

Example

A = a₁, a₂ Lathes are used to produce cylindrical items **such as** shafts or metal cylinders.

Selected Vocabulary

joining processes:

screw   weld
bolt   solder
clamp

joining devices and materials:

a screw   a connector
a bolt   a flange
a nut   a weld
a clamp   solder
a coupling

micrometers:

a micrometer caliper
a depth micrometer
a micrometer cylinder gauge

measurements:

feed   rotary speed
feed speed   cutting speed

Unit 12

Presentation

Read the text and label the flow diagram with sentences a, b, c and d:

Diecasting is a common process in the engineering industry. It is used to produce many machine components. For some metals with a low melting point, such as a zinc alloy, a process called hot-chamber diecasting is used. For example, a carburettor body is produced by this method. There are three main stages in the process. In the first stage the dies are closed. Then the injection plunger is forced downwards and the molten metal is forced into the dies. Finally, in the third stage, the dies are opened in order to remove the carburettor body.

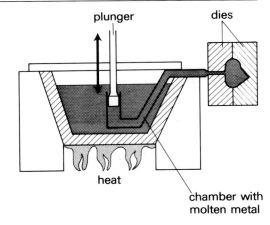

Figure 12.1 Hot-chamber diecasting

Flow diagram

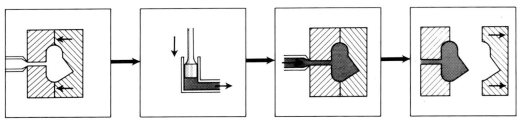

____　____　____　____

a. The dies are opened.
b. The dies are closed.

c. The metal is forced into the dies.
d. The plunger is forced downwards.

Practice 1
Read the text again to complete Table 12.1:

First,	the dies	----	
----	----	----	downwards.
	----	is forced	----
Finally,	----	----	

Table 12.1

40

Practice 2

Complete the flow diagram and the text:

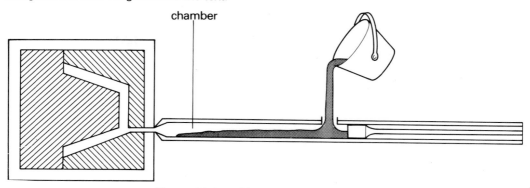

Figure 12.2 Cold-chamber diecasting

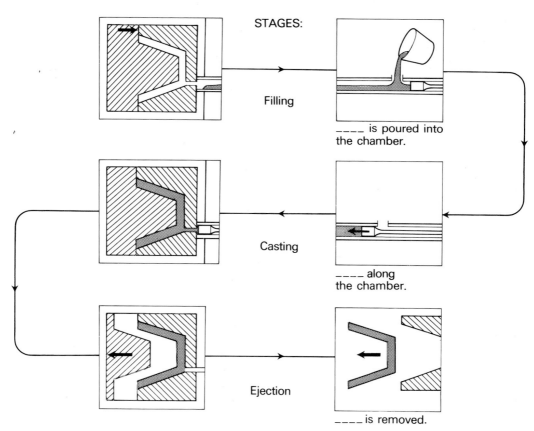

STAGES:

Filling

_____ is poured into
the chamber.

Casting

_____ along
the chamber.

Ejection

_____ is removed.

Figure 12.3 Flow diagram of the process

Cold-chamber diecasting is a suitable
casting process for metals with a high
melting point, such as aluminium. There
are three stages: filling, casting and
ejection. In the first stage, the _____ and
_____. In the casting stage, _____ and _____.
Finally, _____, and the object _____.

Practice 3

Use the first text to complete the second one:

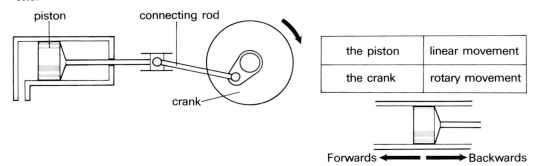

the piston	linear movement
the crank	rotary movement

Forwards ◄━━━━► Backwards

Figure 12.4 Steam engine, piston and crank

In a steam engine, the piston is driven backwards and forwards. This type of movement is called linear movement. In order to convert the linear movement to rotary movement, the piston is connected to a crank by a connecting rod.

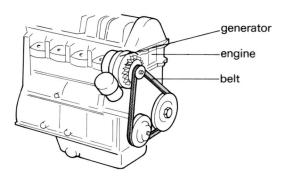

the engine:	rotary movement
the dynamo or alternator:	electrical power

Figure 12.5 Car generator and belt

In a car, the _____ produces _____ movement. In order to _____.

Development

Use the words in the boxes to complete A1–A4 and B1–B5 on pp.43 and 44.

A: The function of components and events

moves downwards		moves up
pushes	mixes	force

B: The stages in the process

is sucked	is ignited
is compressed	are mixed
is converted	are repeated
are pushed	is forced

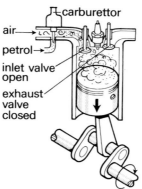

*Figure 12.6
Induction*

A1 First, the carburettor ____ air and petrol together in the correct ratio. Then the piston ____ and sucks the mixture into the cylinder through the inlet valve.

B1 First, air and petrol ____ together. Then the mixture ____ into the cylinder. This is termed the induction stage.

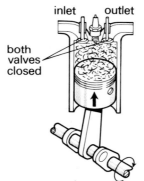

*Figure 12.7
Compression*

A2 The piston then ____ and compresses the mixture.

B2 The mixture ____ . This is called the compression stage.

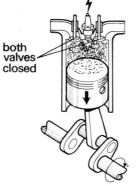

*Figure 12.8
Ignition/
combustion*

A3 The spark plug ignites the compressed mixture. The combustion and rapid expansion of the ignited mixture ____ the piston down. The connecting rod ____ the crankshaft round.

B3 The mixture ____ ; the piston ____ down. The downward linear movement ____ into rotary movement by the piston and crankshaft assembly. This is known as either the ignition or combustion stage.

Unit 12

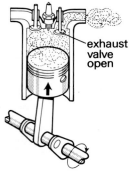

exhaust
valve
open

Figure 12.9
Exhaust

A4 Finally, the piston ____ again to push the burnt gases out through the exhaust valve.

B4 Finally, the exhaust gases ____ out.

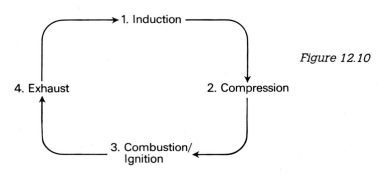

1. Induction

Figure 12.10

4. Exhaust

2. Compression

3. Combustion/ Ignition

B5 The four stages in the 4-stroke cycle ____ again and again.

Summary

Sentence Patterns

In the first stage the dies **are closed**.
Then the mixture **is compressed**.

Finally, the dies **are opened** in order to remove the carburettor body.
Then the mixture **is sucked** into the cylinder.

Connectors

Sequence

A .. B .. C etc. **First** the dies are shaped, **then** the molten metal is poured into the chamber ____.

Finally, the dies are separated.

Selected Vocabulary

process verbs:

force (forced)	compress (-ed)
pour (poured)	push (-ed)
remove (-d)	convert (-ed)
connect (-ed)	repeat (-ed)
produce (-d)	
mix (-ed)	drive (driven)
suck (-ed)	cast (cast)
ignite (-d)	

process nouns:

filling	induction
pouring	compression
casting	ignition
diecasting	combustion
ejection	

44

Unit 13

Presentation

Label Fig. 13.1 and complete Table 13.1:

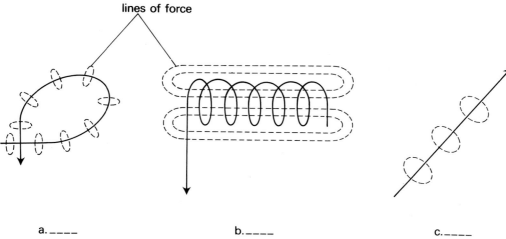

lines of force

a. _ _ _ _   b. _ _ _ _   c. _ _ _ _

Figure 13.1 Magnetic fields

An electric current in a conductor produces a magnetic field. This magnetic field is composed of lines of force. A looped conductor, such as the one in the diagram above, has circular lines of force. Similarly, a straight conductor has circular lines of force, but a much weaker magnetic field. A coiled conductor, such as a coil or a solenoid, has a much stronger magnetic field than a looped conductor or a straight conductor. This is because the lines of force pass through it.

Shape	Lines of force	Strength of magnetic field
straight _ _ _ _	_ _ _ _	_ _ _ _
_ _ _ _	_ _ _ _	_ _ _ _
_ _ _ _	lines of force pass through it.	_ _ _ _

Table 13.1

Practice 1

Complete the text:

The strength of the magnetic field depends on the strength of the current and the shape of _ _ _ _ . For example, a straight conductor has a _ _ _ _ magnetic field than either a looped conductor or _ _ _ _ . Although a looped conductor has a _ _ _ _ magnetic field than a _ _ _ _ , it has a _ _ _ _ than _ _ _ _ .

Practice 2

Use Table 13.2 to complete the sentences:

The table below shows the density and melting point of six common metals.

Metal	Density kg/m^3 (kilograms per metre cubed)	Melting point °C (degrees Celsius)
lead	11 300	600
mild steel	7800	1495
silver	10 500	1230
aluminium	2700	660
copper	8900	1350
zinc	7100	420

Table 13.2

For example:

1 Aluminium has a *lower* density than zinc, but *a slightly higher melting point.*

1 Aluminium has a ____ density than zinc, but _____ .

2 Copper has ____ density than silver, but _____ .

3 Lead has ____ melting point than aluminium, but _____ .

4 Mild steel has ____ density than copper, but _____ .

5 Silver ____ than lead, but _____ .

6 Lead ____ mild steel, _____ .

Development

Use Table 13.3 to complete the text:

Moving-coil meters and moving-iron meters are both electromagnetic devices. They are commonly used as voltmeters and ammeters in electrical engineering. They are simple devices and there are some differences between them.

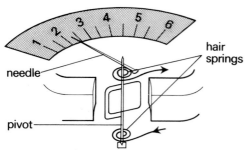

Figure 13.2 Moving-coil meter

The moving-coil meter is an expensive and delicate type of measuring instrument. It measures only a.c., and has

a ____ sensitivity. As shown in the figure, it has ____ scale divisions. The main parts consist of a coil ____ and _____. The current enters and leaves the coil via ____. When the current is switched on, the coil _____.

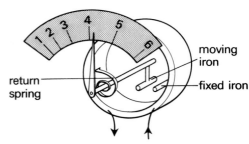

Figure 13.3 Moving-iron meter

The moving-iron meter is an ____ and robust type of measuring instrument. It measures both ____, and has a lower ____ than _____. Unlike the moving-coil meter, it has ____ divisions. The main parts _____. When the current _____, the magnets _____.

	Moving-coil type	Moving-iron type
Current	a.c. (alternating current)	a.c. and d.c. (direct current)
Price	expensive	inexpensive
Sensitivity	high	low
Scale divisions	equal	unequal
Main parts	coil on a frame, 2 hair springs	coil round 2 magnets, return spring
Magnetic action	coil pivots between 2 magnets	magnets repel each other

Table 13.3 Comparison of the two meters

Summary

Connectors

Similarity

$\left.\begin{matrix} A \\ B \end{matrix}\right\} = X$ A looped conductor has circular lines of force. **Similarly**, a straight conductor has circular lines of force.
Looped conductors and straight conductors **both** have circular lines of force.

Difference

$A \neq B$ **Unlike** the moving-coil meter, the moving-iron meter has unequal scale divisions.

$A\,(-)$; **Although** a looped conductor
$B\,(+)$ has a stronger magnetic field than a straight conductor, it has a weaker magnetic field than a coiled conductor.

Reference

A coiled conductor has a much stronger magnetic field ; **this is because** the lines of force pass through it.

Fig. 13.2. **As shown in the diagram,** the moving-coil meter has equal scale divisions.

Selected Vocabulary

electrical concepts:

lines of force
a magnetic field
strength of current

properties:

expensive
inexpensive
delicate
robust
simple

electrical components:

a looped conductor   a coil
a coiled conductor   a solenoid
an electromagnetic device   a voltmeter
a moving-coil meter   an ammeter
a moving-iron meter

measurement:

density   a.c. (alternating current)
melting-point   d.c. (direct current)
sensitivity

structure/composition:

(The meter) **consists of** (a coil, a frame and two hair springs).
(A magnetic field) **is composed of** (lines of force).

verbs of motion:

pass (-ed)   repel (-led)
enter (-ed)   leave (left)
pivot (-ed)

Unit 14

Presentation

Read the text and label the drawings with
instructions a, b, c, d, or e:

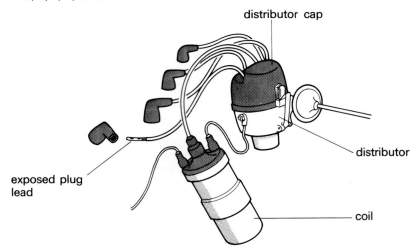

distributor cap

distributor

exposed plug
lead

coil

Figure 14.1 The ignition system

The coil produces high-tension electrical
power. The distributor transmits this
power to the spark plugs.
To check the ignition system follow these
steps:

1 Remove the cap from one of the plug
  leads.
2 Hold the exposed end close to a good
  earth, e.g. an engine bolt.
3 Switch on the ignition.
4 Turn the engine.
5 Check for a spark as follows:
  a. If there is a spark between the plug
     lead and the earth, there is no fault.
  b. If there is no spark, check the
     electrical circuit in the distributor.
  c. To check the distributor, use an
     insulated screwdriver.
     Hold it against a good earth
     conductor and close to the
     distributor brush.
  d. If there is a spark, the fault is in the
     distributor. Check its condition.
  e. If there is no spark, check the coil.

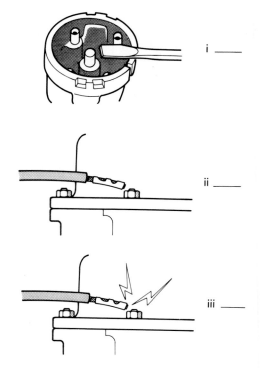

i ____

ii ____

iii ____

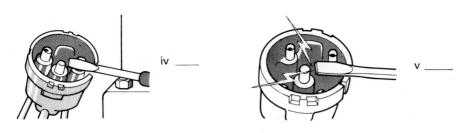

Practice 1
Complete Table 14.1:

Observation	Action
No spark between the plug lead and the earth	Check ____
____ between ____ and ____	Check the condition of the distributor
Spark between ____ and ____	No action
____ between ____	Check the coil

Table 14.1

Practice 2
Complete the instructions on the next page with a, b, c, d and e:

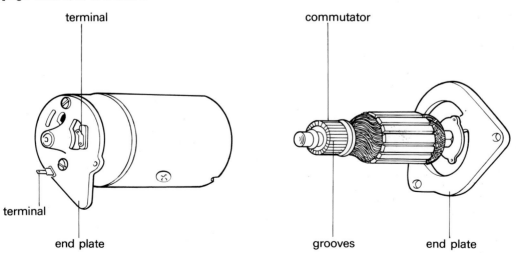

Figure 14.2 Repairing a generator

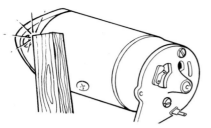

1 If the end plate does not come off, ____.

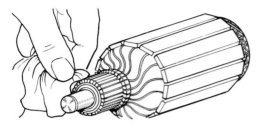

2 ____, clean it with a petrol-moistened cloth.

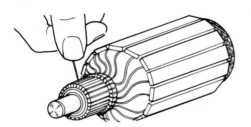

3 ____, clean them with a pin.

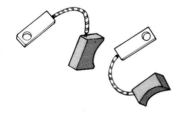

4 If the brushes are worn, ____.

5 ____, use a small file to clean them.

a. replace them.
b. If the commutator is dirty,
c. If the terminals are rusty,
d. tap it with a piece of wood.
e. If the grooves on the commutator are clogged

Practice 3

Use the diagrams to complete the text and the table:

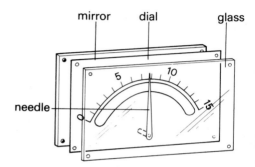

Figure 14.3 The main parts of a dial

Some measuring instruments are fitted with dials. To prevent incorrect readings, always read the dial correctly. Read the dial from directly in front so that the reflection is behind the needle. If the dial is not viewed from the front the reading will be incorrect.

viewing position	reading
from the ____ from the ____ from the ____	correct high low

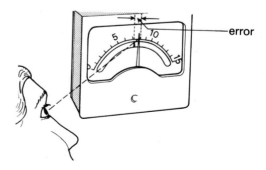

If the instrument is viewed from the left, the reading will be ____ .

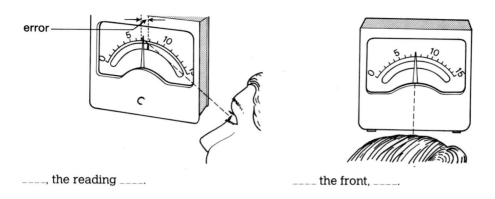

____, the reading ____.

____ the front, ____.

Development

Use Figs. 14.4 and 14.5 to complete the text:

Voltage is stepped up or stepped down by means of a transformer. This apparatus is shown in Fig. 14.4.

If a current is passed through the primary winding, a current is induced in the secondary winding. This is known as mutual induction. The strength of the induced current in the secondary winding depends on the number of turns on the secondary winding.

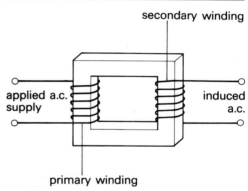

Figure 14.4 Transformer principle

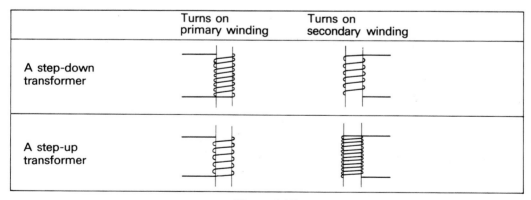

Figure 14.5

A step-down transformer
If the number of turns on the primary winding is more than the number of turns on ____, the induced voltage will be less than ____ voltage.

A step-up transformer
If the number of turns on ____ is more than ____

Unit 14

Summary

Sentence Patterns

If the end plate does not come off, **tap** it with a piece of wood.

If there is a spark between the plug lead and earth, **there is** no fault.

If the dial is viewed from the left, the reading **will be** high.

Reference

Check for a spark **as follows**: 1 ____ 2 ____ 3 ____.

If the brushes are worn, replace **them**.

If the terminals are rusty, use a small file to clean **them**.

Selected Vocabulary

tools:

a screwdriver
an insulated screwdriver
a file

electrical components and devices:

a spark plug	a brush
a distributor	a commutator
	a transformer

instructions:

check	follow
hold	clean
tap	replace
fit	view
read	switch on

other electrical terminology:

mutual induction	primary winding
induced voltage	secondary winding
applied voltage	

Unit 15

Presentation

Read the text and complete the tree diagram in Fig. 15.1:

The raw materials for plastics are coal and oil, and many plastic materials today are produced from oil. Plastics can be divided into two main categories. The first group, called thermoplastics, includes well-known plastics such as PVC, nylon and polythene. These can be treated (heated, softened and cooled) several times, and can be formed into combs, pipes and bags, in addition to many other similar products.

Thermosetting plastics include melamine, polyurethane and phenolic resin, and can be made into tableware, foams and plugs respectively. However, this group differs from thermoplastics because they can be treated only once and harden when they are heated.

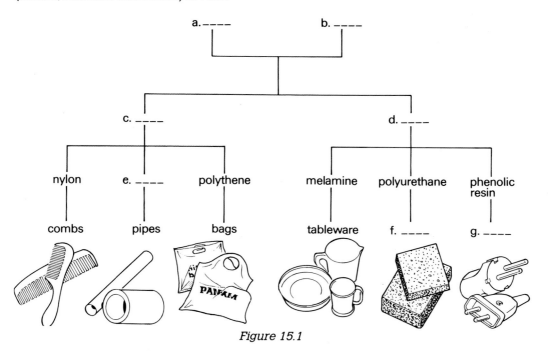

a. ----   b. ----

c. ----   d. ----

nylon   e. ----   polythene   melamine   polyurethane   phenolic resin

combs   pipes   bags   tableware   f. ----   g. ----

Figure 15.1

Practice 1

Complete the sentences:

1 Nylon is a thermoplastic, and it ____ into combs.
2 Phenolic resin is a ____, and it ____.
3 Melamine and polyurethane are examples of ____, and they can be formed into ____ and ____ respectively.
4 Products such as ____ and bags ____ from PVC and ____ respectively.
5 ____ can be treated more than once, whereas ____ harden when they are treated; therefore they ____ only once.

Unit 15

Practice 2

Complete the passage by using Table 15.1.

		screw threads
	Mechanical	rivets
		soldering
Joining methods	Thermal	brazing
		welding
	Adhesive	

Table 15.1

Metals can be joined by three basic methods: mechanical, thermal and ____. Both the mechanical and ____ methods can be further divided. The former method ____ screw threads and ____, and the latter method can be broken down into ____.

Practice 3

Read the text and complete Table 15.2:
Use these symbols: ✓ (yes)   × (no)

Metal	Properties				Uses
	Ductile	Malleable	Corrosion resistant	Good conductor of electricity	
cast iron				×	machine castings
wrought iron				×	----
lead	✓		✓		----
tin			✓		coating for steel
copper					----

Table 15.2 Properties of metals

Metals are used for a variety of engineering purposes, depending on the properties of the metals. Certain common metals have malleable and ductile properties. If a metal is malleable it can be hammered or pressed into a new shape. Copper is a good example of this. It is also a ductile metal because it can be stretched into another shape. Lead also has these properties, although it is less ductile than copper.

Whereas copper is a good conductor of electricity and is frequently used for electrical conductors, lead is not. Lead can be used for the sheaths on electrical cables. Lead, like copper and tin, will resist corrosion.

Tin and wrought iron can be stretched, and also have malleable properties. The former is corrosion resistant, but wrought iron easily corrodes. Wrought iron can be used for chains and crane hooks. Neither of these two metals is a good conductor of electricity.

Cast iron is unlike the other metals because its shape cannot be altered by hammering, pressing or stretching, and it is not corrosion resistant.

Practice 4

Complete the sentences and label the drawings with a, b and c:

a. A ductile metal such as ____ can be ____.

b. ____ is an example of a malleable metal because ____.

c. Unlike cast iron, ____ is corrosion resistant.

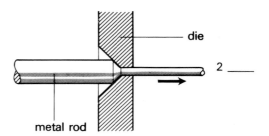

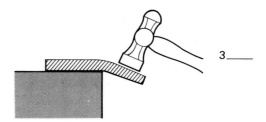

Development

Use the tree diagram in Fig. 15.2 to complete the text:

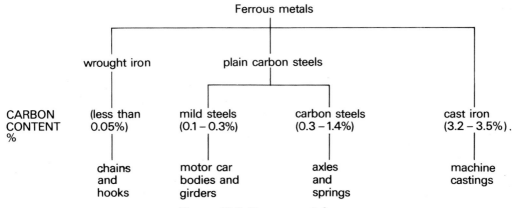

Figure 15.2 Ferrous metals

Ferrous metals are based on iron. They are usually alloyed with carbon because it increases the strength of iron and makes it much more useful to the engineer. Slight variations in the carbon content can make very great differences in the properties of the metal. Wrought iron is a ferrous metal with a carbon content of less than 0.05%. Chains and hooks can be produced from this alloy.

There are two groups of ____: mild steels have ____ and carbon steels ____. Cast iron ____

Summary

Sentence Patterns

Thermoplastics **can be treated** *several times.*
Metals **can be joined** *by three basic methods.*

Connectors

Addition

A + B   These can be formed into combs, pipes and bags **in addition to** many other products.

Similarity

A = B   Copper, **like** tin, can resist corrosion.

Reference

Tin and wrought iron can be stretched. **Neither** of these two metals is a good conductor.

Tin and wrought iron have malleable properties. **The former** is corrosion resistant.

Tin and wrought iron have malleable properties. **The latter** corrodes easily.

Tin and wrought iron can be stretched. **The former** is corrosion resistant but the **latter** corrodes easily.

Selected Vocabulary

types of joint:
mechanical
thermal
adhesive
soldered
welded
brazed
} joints

joining processes:
soldering
welding
brazing
riveting

manufacturing processes:
heating   hammering
cooling   pressing
softening   stretching
hardening

properties:
malleable
ductile
corrosion resistant

materials:
coal   cast iron
oil   wrought iron
plastics   carbon steels
nylon   mild steels

Unit 16

Presentation

Give each part of Fig. 16.1 the correct
instruction:

a. Before soldering, the wires must be
   marked and the insulation sleeves
   must be put on the wires.
b. Push the insulation sleeves over the
   soldered connections.
c. Strip the outer insulation.
d. The wires must be soldered to the
   correct tags.
e. Strip the ends of the wires with a wire
   stripper.

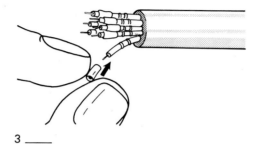

3 ____

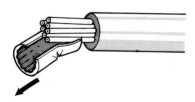

1 ____

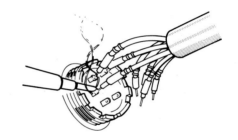

4 ____

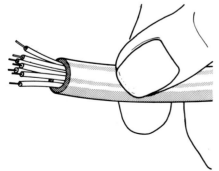

2 ____

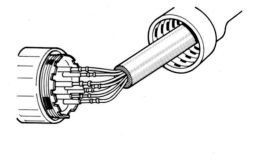

5 ____

Figure 16.1 Soldering a multicore wire

57

Unit 16

Practice 1

Use the diagrams in Fig. 16.2 and Fig. 16.3 to complete the texts:

The electrical system in a car can have either a positive or a negative earth. In both systems, the battery leads and terminals must be connected correctly. The diagrams in Fig. 16.2 and Fig. 16.3 below show the two electrical systems.

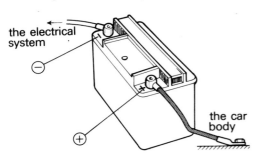
the electrical system

the car body

Figure 16.2 System for a car with a positive earth

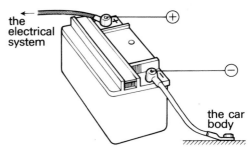
the electrical system

the car body

Figure 16.3 System for a car with a negative earth

In a car with a ____, the positive terminal must be connected to ____.
The negative terminal must ____ to the ____.

In a car with a ____ earth, the positive terminal ____.
The negative ____.

Practice 2

Label the pictures and symbols in Fig. 16.4 with a, b, c, d, e and f. Complete warnings d and e.

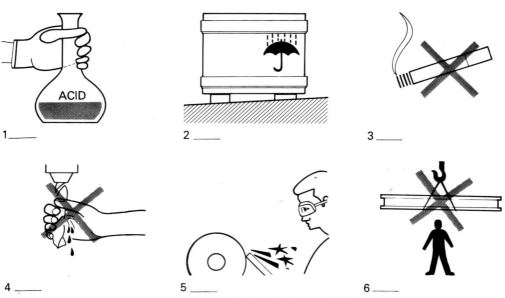

1 ____   2 ____   3 ____

4 ____   5 ____   6 ____

Figure 16.4 Safety in the workshop

a. Always wear rubber gloves.
b. Never stand under a suspended load.
c. No smoking.
d. ____ wear gloves when operating a drilling machine.

e. ____ protect the eyes when operating a grinding wheel.
f. Protect from water.

Practice 3

Complete the warnings with a, b, c, d and e:

1 ____ when operating a grinding wheel.

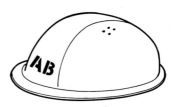

4 ____ when working with overhead loads.

2 ____ when working with electrical cables.

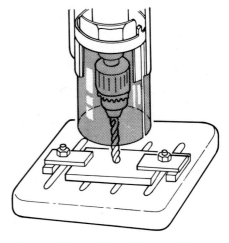

5 Guards must be positioned correctly ____.

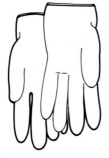

3 Rubber gloves must be worn ____.

a. when handling acidic substances.
b. A mask or goggles must be worn
c. Helmets must be worn
d. when operating machines.
e. The electricity supply must be switched off

Figure 16.5 Safety in the workshop

Unit 16

Practice 4
Complete these warnings:

To protect the eyes, goggles must ____.
To protect the head, ____.
To prevent electric shocks, ____.
To ____ burns to the hands, ____.

Development

Use Table 16.1 to complete the text:

	Method	Prevention
treated paper	wrapping	corrosion and knocking
plastic dip	dipping	damage to threads
anti corrosion fluid	spraying	corrosion
separators	stacking	scratching and marking
grease	smearing	corrosion

Table 16.1 Materials protection

Finished parts are easily damaged by chemical action (corrosion) and mechanical damage (abrasion, scraping and marking etc.). Therefore, after production, finished parts must be protected against such damage.

Small parts must be put in containers to prevent movement, and larger parts must be stacked with ____ between them to prevent ____.

Precision parts ____ in hot plastic to ____. Iron and steel particularly must ____ against corrosion in one of three ways. They can be ____, sprayed with ____ or ____.

Unit 16

Summary

Sentence Patterns

Precision parts **must be protected**.
Goggles **must be worn**.

Precision parts **must be protected** *against damage*.
Rubber gloves **must be worn** *when handling acidic substances*.

Connectors

Sequence

A(2) ← B(1)   **Before** soldering (2), the wire must be marked (1).

A(1) → B(2)   **After** production, finished parts must be protected.

A ⎫ →
B ⎭ →   Rubber gloves must be worn **when** handling acids.

Selected Vocabulary

safety equipment:

goggles
a mask
a helmet
gloves
a guard

activities and processes:

marking	smearing
stripping	spraying
stacking	protection
dipping	corrosion
wrapping	

verbs:

mark (-ed)	spray (-ed)
strip (-ped)	protect (-ed)
stack (-ed)	corrode (-d)
dip (-ped)	keep (kept)
wrap (-ped)	stand (stood)
smear (-ed)	wear (worn)

tools and machines:

a wire stripper
a grinding wheel
a drilling machine

Unit 17

Presentation

Read the text and tick (√) the type of joint recommended in Table 17.1:

Figure 17.1

Riveting is a method of joining metals permanently. The process consists of drilling or punching the metal plates, inserting the rivet and then closing it by compression force.

There are several standard types of rivet heads with different uses. Flat head rivets should be used for joints where little strength is required; countersunk and mushroom head rivets are both recommended for joints where a flush surface is required, though mushroom head rivets should be used for joints which must also be strong. Roundhead and pan head rivets are recommended for joints which must be very strong; the latter are exceptionally strong and are therefore used in heavy constructional engineering.

		Not strong	Strong	Very strong	Exceptionally strong	Flush surface
Countersunk						
Pan head						
Flat head						
Mushroom						
Roundhead						

Table 17.1 Rivet type and joints

Practice 1

Use Table 17.1 to complete the sentences.
For example:

1 *Countersunk rivets should be used for* joints which must be flush.

or

Countersunk rivets are recommended for joints which must be flush.

1 ____ for joints which must be flush.

2 ____ for joints where little strength is required.

3 ____ for joints which must be both flush and strong.

4 ____ for joints where exceptional strength is required.

5 ____ for joints which must be very strong.

Practice 2

Use Table 17.2 to complete the text:

Material	Property		Examples of uses
Cast iron	500 k — cast iron component	Compressive strength (strong in compression)	Machine beds Machine frames
Wrought iron	wrought iron component 100 k	Tensile strength (strong in tension)	Crane hooks Railway couplings
Mild steel	mild steel component	Shear strength (strong in shear)	Rivets Bolts
Medium carbon steel	medium carbon steel component	Impact strength (tough)	Axles Hammer heads

Table 17.2 Material properties

For example:

Cast iron should be used for components which *must be strong in compression.* It is recommended for *machine beds and frames.*

Wrought iron is recommended for components where *tensile strength is required;* for example, *crane hooks and railway couplings.*

Cast iron should be used for components which ____. It is recommended for ____.

Wrought iron is recommended for components where ____; for example, ____.

Mild steel should be used for components which ____, therefore it is recommended for ____.

Medium carbon steel is recommended for components where ____; for example, ____.

Unit 17

Development

Use Figs. 17.2, 17.3, and 17.4 to complete the text. Read it through first.

____ are not recommended for soft-soldered joints. ____ should be used because of their greater surface area (see Fig. 17.2). Similarly, ____ should be used rather than ____ (see Fig. 17.3). Where a really strong joint is required, ____ are recommended rather than ____ (see Fig. 17.4).

A simple T-butt joint

Figure 17.2

A folded T-butt joint

A straight butt joint

Figure 17.3

A simple butt joint with cover strap

A simple lap joint

Figure 17.4

An interlocking joint

Summary

Sentence Patterns

Flathead rivets **should be used** *for joints where little strength is required.*

Roundhead rivets **are recommended** *for joints which must be very strong.*
Simple T-butt and straight butt joints **are not recommended** *for soft-soldered joints.*

Connectors

Preference

A (√); B (×)   Folded T-butt joints should be used **rather than** simple T-butt joints.

Reference

Countersunk rivets should be used for joints **which** must be flush.
Wrought iron is recommended for components **where** tensile strength is required.

Selected Vocabulary

properties:

tensile strength	— strong in tension
compressive strength	— strong in compression
shear strength	— strong in shear
impact strength	— tough

types of rivet: (see Table 17.1).

types of joint: (see Figs. 17.2, 17.3, 17.4)

Unit 18

Presentation

Read the text. Put ticks ($\checkmark$) or crosses ($\times$) next to the beams in Table 18.1. Use this system: $\checkmark$ = safe
$\checkmark\checkmark$ = very safe
$\times\times$ = very unsafe

Before cutting holes and notches in beams, a structural engineer should always be consulted. Although holes and notches should never be cut in concrete beams, they can be cut in metal beams. The holes should lie along the point of minimum stress (i.e. the neutral axis) and be as small as possible. However the flanges of metal beams should never be notched as this is the point of maximum stress. To be completely safe, it is advisable to attach the pipework to the beam by means of saddles.

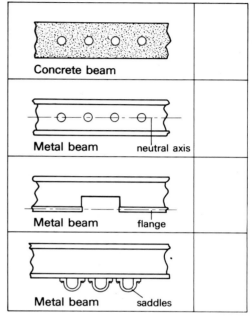

Table 18.1 Holes and notches in beams

Practice 1

Use the information in Table 18.2 to complete the sentences:

For example:

1 1.5 mm rivets *should always be punched at least* 3 mm from the edge.
2 4.0 mm rivets *should never be punched more than* 96 mm apart.

1   1.5 mm rivets ____ 3 mm from the edge.
2   4.0 mm rivets ____ 96 mm apart.

3   8.0 mm rivets ____ 80 mm from the edge.
4   9.5 mm rivets ____ 28.5 mm apart.
5   3.0 mm rivets ____ 72 mm apart.
6   1.5 mm rivets ____ 15 mm from the edge.
7   9.5 mm rivets ____ 19 mm from the edge.
8   8.0 mm rivets ____ 24 mm apart.

Edge distance:	2 × diameter of rivet (minimum)
	10 × diameter of rivet (maximum)
Spacing between rivets:	3 × diameter of rivet (minimum)
	24 × diameter of rivet (maximum)

Table 18.2 Positioning of rivets

Practice 2
Use Table 18.3 to complete the text:

	Ease of production				Application
	Very easy	Easy	Difficult	Very difficult	
V-thread	✓				Most screw fastening
Square thread			✓		Machine lead screws
Knuckle thread		✓			Railway couplings
Acme thread				✓	Lead screws with split nut

Table 18.3 Screw threads

In Table 18.3, there are 4 common types of screw threads. The V-thread is the ____ to produce and is suitable for ____. The Acme thread is the ____ to produce but is suitable for ____. The Knuckle thread is ____ to produce than the Square thread and is used where rough and heavy wear will occur, for example for ____. The Square thread is recommended for ____.

Development

Use the information in Table 18.4 to recommend the most suitable method of joining for the jobs illustrated in Fig. 18.1.

Joining methods	Applications
1 Screw fastening	Temporary assembly joints
2 Riveting	Permanent thin sheet-metal joints
3 Soldering	Permanent small and weak joints
4 Brazing	Permanent strong, medium-sized joints
5 Welding	Permanent, very strong large-scale joints
6 Using Adhesives	Permanent joints between two dissimilar materials

Table 18.4

Unit 18

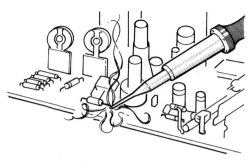

a. Making connections in electrical circuits: method ____

d. Fitting a maintenance cover to drains: method ____

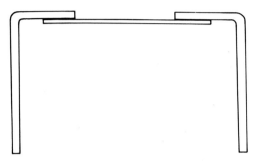

b. Joining metal sheets to an outer metal casing: method ____

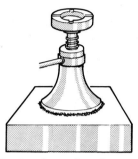

e. Joining hydraulic jack to base: method ____

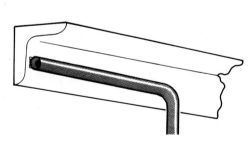

c. Joining a nylon tube to metal structure: method ____

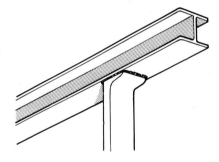

f. Joining steel support girder to steel beam: method ____

Figure 18.1

Now complete the text below:

____ is recommended for making connections on electrical circuits but it should never be used where strong joints are required. For permanent joints between two dissimilar materials like nylon and metal, it is advisable to use ____. For temporary jobs like fitting a maintenance cover ____ should always be used. ____ is recommended for permanent sheet-metal joints such as outer casing fittings. Although ____ should always be used for steel support girders, ____ can be used for medium-sized joints where strength is required; for example the joint between the base and body of a hydraulic jack.

67

Unit 18

Summary

Sentence Patterns

It **is** advisable to attach the pipework *by means of saddles.*
For joints between dissimilar materials, it **is** advisable to use adhesives.
Holes and notches **should** *never* **be cut** *in concrete beams.*

Connectors

Exemplification

A (= a₁)   For permanent joints between two dissimilar materials **like** nylon and metal, it is advisable to use adhesive.

Selected Vocabulary

structural engineering:
  the neutral axis
  the point of minimum stress
  the point of maximum stress
  concrete beams
  metal beams
  saddles
  support girders
  pipework
  a notch
  a hole
  a flange

screw thread types: (see Table 18.3)

joint properties:
  permanent
  temporary
  large-scale
  medium-sized

quantity/size:
  minimum
  maximum
  at least

Unit 19

Presentation

Read the text and identify the three
furnaces illustrated in Fig. 19.1:

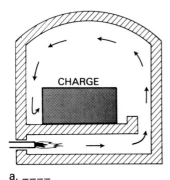
a. ____

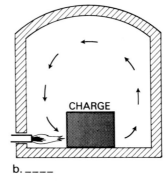
b. ____

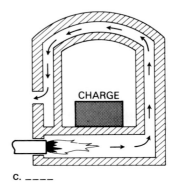
c. ____

Figure 19.1 Heat treatment in three furnaces

The open hearth furnace is the simplest
form of furnace. The heat is produced by a
gas or oil burner which plays directly onto
the charge. The heat circulates around the
furnace and is reflected back onto the
charge by the lining.

The semi-muffle furnace is an
improvement on the open hearth furnace in
that the flame does not play directly onto

the charge. Bottom heat is provided by
conduction from the hearth and additional
heat is provided by circulation of flue
gases.

The muffle furnace is the most efficient of
these three. The charge is separated from
the combustion chamber so that the heat
circulates around the outer chamber and
the gases flow out through the flue outlet.

Practice 1

Use Fig. 19.1 to complete the sentences
with the words in the box below:

does not play	plays
is separated	is not separated
is not provided	is provided

For example:

1 In the muffle furnace the charge *is
separated* from the combustion
chamber.

1 In the muffle furnace the charge ____
from the combustion chamber.
2 In the open hearth furnace the flame
____ directly onto the charge.
3 In the semi-muffle furnace the charge
____ from the combustion chamber.
4 Bottom heat ____ in the muffle furnace.
5 In the muffle furnace the flame ____
directly onto the charge.
6 Bottom heat ____ in the open hearth
furnace.

Practice 2

Look at these two sentences:

> The heat is produced by a gas or oil burner.
> The gas or oil burner plays directly onto the charge.

Find the above information in the text about furnaces.

There is only one sentence:

> 'The heat is produced by a gas or oil burner **which** plays directly onto the charge.'

Now join these sentences:

1 In the semi-muffle furnace heat is produced by a gas or oil burner.
   The gas or oil burner does not play directly onto the charge.

2 In the semi-muffle furnace heat is produced by a gas or oil burner.
   The gas or oil burner provides bottom heat.

3 In the muffle furnace the charge is separated from the combustion chamber.
   The combustion chamber is heated by a gas or oil burner.

Practice 3

Use Table 19.1 to complete the descriptions below:

+ = positive feature
− = negative feature

	Open hearth	Semi-muffle	Muffle
Price	+	+	−
Operation	+	+	−
Economy (fuel)	+	+	−
Even heating	−	−	+
Temperature control	−	+	+
Atmosphere control	−	−	+

Table 19.1

For example:

The open hearth furnace is the simplest form of furnace. It is cheap, simple to operate and economical. However, it does not heat evenly, it does not have good temperature control or good atmosphere control.

The semi-muffle furnace is an improvement on the open hearth furnace. It _____.

The muffle furnace is the most efficient of these three furnaces. It _____.

Unit 19

Development

Read the text to complete Table 19.2:

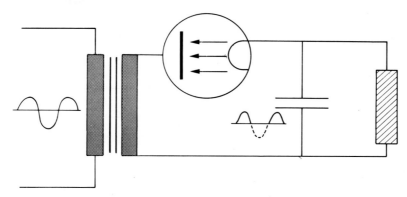

Figure 19.2 One-way rectifier tube

A rectifier is a device which allows an electric current to pass in one direction but not in the opposite direction. There are various types of rectifier. Four of the most common are described below: Selenium rectifiers, which are made of an aluminium plate with a selenium coating, are used for high power rectification. Instrument rectifiers are normally of the copper oxide type, which consist of a copper disc with a cuprous oxide coating. Semi-conductor diodes, which are made with germanium or silicon, are suitable for all power rectification, but are particularly useful for the low to medium power range. Thermionic diodes, which are found in radio circuits, consist of two electrodes in a vacuum.

Rectifier type	Composition	Properties	Applications
Selenium rectifier		Large and heavy but capable of high power rectification	
Copper oxide rectifier		Large and heavy but with high and stable reverse resistance	
Semi-conductor diodes		Small and robust	
Thermionic diodes		Small and very effective at low currents	

Table 19.2

Now use Table 19.2 to complete the text below:

____, which are made from either germanium or silicon, are used for all ____, especially ____. Their small size and robust nature make them the most efficient of all rectifiers. ____, which consist of 2 electrodes in a vacuum, are found in ____ because they ____, ____ and ____ are both metal rectifiers. The former consists of ____ and the latter ____. Although metal rectifiers are not so efficient as either ____ or ____, they have important applications. Selenium rectifiers are used for ____. ____ rectifiers are suitable as instrument rectifiers because ____.

Summary

Sentence Patterns

The heat **is produced** by a burner *which plays directly onto the charge.*
A rectifier **is** a device *which allows a current to flow in one direction only.*

In a semi-muffle furnace, the flame **does not play** *directly onto the charge.*
In the open-hearth furnace, the charge **is not separated** *from the combustion chamber.*

Thermionic diodes, which are found in radio circuits, **consist of** two electrodes in a vacuum.
Thermionic diodes, which consist of two electrodes in a vacuum, **are found** in radio circuits.

Connectors

Purpose

A → B   The charge is separated from the combustion chamber **so that** the heat circulates around the outer chamber.

Reference

| Semi-conductor diodes |, **which** are made with germanium or silicon, are suitable for all power rectification. **Their** small size and robust nature make them the most efficient of all rectifiers.

Selected Vocabulary

qualities:

efficient	even
cheap	effective
economical	stable

electrical terminology:

a rectifier	rectification
a diode	low power range
an electrode	medium power range
	high power range

useful verbs:

provide (-d)	circulate (-d)
reflect (-ed)	allow (-ed)
produce (-d)	pass (-ed)
separate (-d)	find (found)
play (-ed)	
heat (-ed)	

types of furnace: (see Fig. 19.1)

Unit 20

Presentation

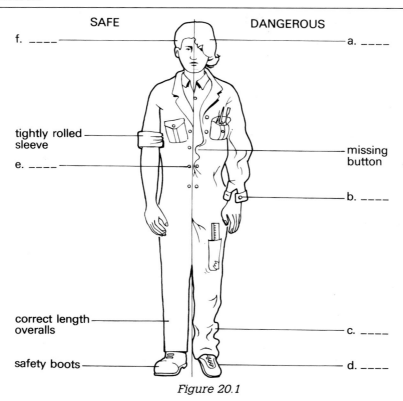

SAFE   DANGEROUS

f. ____

a. ____

tightly rolled sleeve

missing button

e. ____

b. ____

correct length overalls

c. ____

safety boots

d. ____

Figure 20.1

Read the safety warnings below.
Complete the labelling of Fig. 20.1.

Always keep hair short since long hair can be caught in moving machinery.

Fasten all buttons as loose clothing can be caught in moving machinery.

Feet can easily be injured when lightweight shoes are worn.

Sleeves should always be rolled up because loose cuffs can catch in moving machinery.

Falls can easily occur when overalls are too long.

Practice 1

Use *because* to complete the sentences:

For example:

1 Lightweight shoes *are dangerous because feet can easily be injured.*

1 Lightweight shoes ____.
2 Loose cuffs ____.
3 Long overalls ____.
4 Long hair ____.
5 Loose clothing ____.

Practice 2

First use the information in Table 18.2 on page 65 to complete Table 20.1:

Metal thickness	Rivet diameter	Minimum edge distance	Minimum rivet spacing
0.80 mm	1.5 mm	----	----
1.25 mm	3.2 mm	----	----
2.50 mm	4.8 mm	----	----
4.80 mm	9.5 mm	----	----

Table 20.1

Now use Table 20.1 to complete the fault diagnosis in Table 20.2:

Fault		Cause
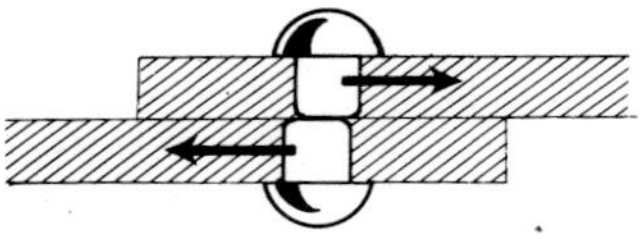	Shearing of the rivet MT = 1.25 mm RD = 2.9 mm	The rivet diameter is too ----
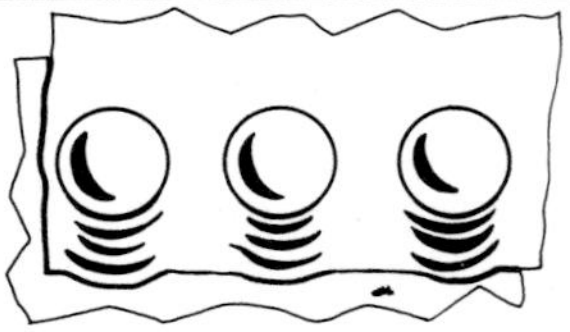	Crushing of the metal MT = 2.50 mm RD = 5.2 mm	The rivet diameter is too ----
	Splitting of the metal RD = 3.2 mm ED = 4.8 mm	The rivets are too ----
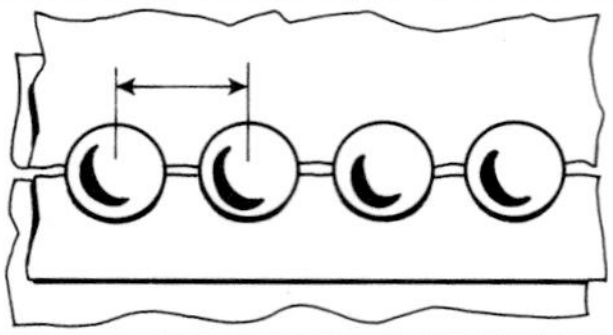	Tearing of the plate RD = 9.5 mm RS = 14 mm	The rivets are too ----
MT : Metal thickness RD : Rivet diameter	ED : Edge distance RS : Rivet spacing	

Table 20.2 Rivet faults

☐ The invar strip is pulled inwards.

1 *The iron is switched on.*

☐ The inner contact spring pushes against the outer contact spring.

☐ The element is switched off.

☐ The circuit is made.

☐ The temperature of the intermediate plate decreases.

☐ The element reaches the required temperature.

☐ The connecting rod pushes against the inner contact spring.

☐ The heating element is switched on again.

☐ The intermediate plate contracts.

2 *The heating element is heated to the required temperature.*

☐ The iron cools.

Summary

Sentence Patterns

Expansion **causes** the bimetal strip to bend.

Connectors

Result

A ∴ B The intermediate plate contracts. **Consequently** the invar strip is pulled inwards.

A ∴ B The temperature of the intermediate plate decreases, **thereby** causing it to contract.

Sequence

A→B→ **Once** the iron reaches the required temperature, the element is switched off.

Reference

The strips are usually made of ⊏ brass ⊐ (**an alloy of copper and zinc**) .. and ⊏ invar ⊐, **a ferrous alloy** ..

The bimetal strip consists of two dissimilar ⊏ strips of metal ⊐, **welded together**.

Selected Vocabulary

thermostatic control:

expand (-ed)	reduce (-d)
increase (-d)	activate (-d)
contract (-ed)	decrease (-d)

changes:

expansion	an increase
contraction	a decrease
	a reduction

other useful words:

a liquid	a spring
a thermostat	a load
a contact	an element

Unit 22

Presentation

Read the text and label Fig. 22.1:

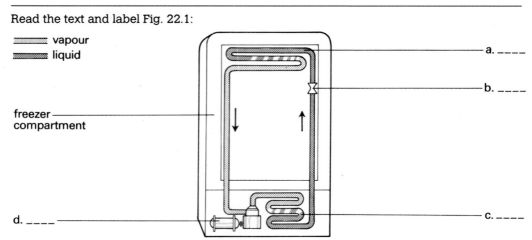

vapour
liquid

freezer compartment

a. _ _ _ _

b. _ _ _ _

c. _ _ _ _

d. _ _ _ _

Figure 22.1 A compression refrigerator

The refrigerant, which is under low pressure, is evaporated in the evaporator. The latter is a coiled pipe mounted in the freezer compartment. The evaporation leads to a drop in temperature in the freezer compartment. A small compressor draws away the vapour, compresses it and passes it to a condenser, where heat is given off. As a result of increased pressure and loss of heat, the refrigerant condenses. Finally, the now liquid refrigerant expands, after passing through an expansion valve, and consequently the pressure drops. The refrigerant is now returned to the evaporator.

Practice 1

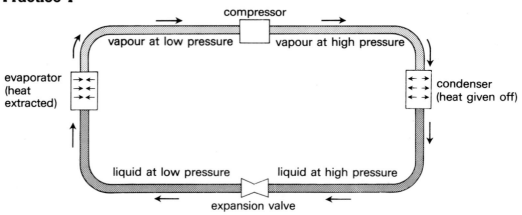

compressor

vapour at low pressure

vapour at high pressure

evaporator (heat extracted)

condenser (heat given off)

liquid at low pressure

liquid at high pressure

expansion valve

Figure 22.2 Operating principle of a compression refrigerator

Use Fig. 22.2 to match the causes with the effects in Table 22.1.

Cause	Effect
Evaporation	Vapour changes into a liquid
Compression	Vapour increases in pressure
Condensation	Liquid changes into a vapour
Expansion	Liquid decreases in pressure

Table 22.1

Practice 2
Use Table 22.2 to complete the text:

Refrigerants	Properties
Water	Slow evaporation
Ether	Very fast evaporation Poisonous Inflammable
Freon	Fast evaporation Non-toxic Non-flammable

Table 22.2

Water is not used in refrigerators because it _____. Ether, another refrigerant, is never used in domestic refrigerators since _____. However, it is sometimes used for industrial refrigeration because _____. Freon is usually used in domestic refrigerators as _____.

Development

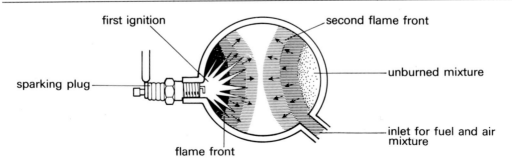

first ignition

second flame front

sparking plug

unburned mixture

flame front

inlet for fuel and air mixture

Figure 22.3 The combustion process in a petrol engine

Read the text and then complete Table 22.3.

A petrol and air mixture is drawn into the cylinder, compressed and ignited by a spark. First, the petrol and air mixture ignites near the spark. Then, heat given off by the burning fuel particles causes adjacent particles to ignite. Consequently, a flame front spreads through the combustion chamber.

As a result of thermal radiation, increased pressure and hot pockets in the combustion chamber, a second ignition and flame front may occur in the unburned mixture. Sometimes this may lead to violent combustion of the unburned mixture, causing knocking in the engine.

Cause	Effects
Heat given off by burning fuel particles	1 ____ 2 a flame front spreads through the combustion chamber
Thermal radiation, ____ and ____	1 a second ignition and flame front 2 ____ → 3 ____

Table 22.3

Summary

Sentence Patterns

As a result of increased pressure, the refrigerant **condenses**.
Evaporation **leads to** a drop in temperature.

Ether **is** *sometimes* **used** *for industrial refrigeration*.
Freon **is** *usually* **used** *in domestic refrigerators*.

This **may lead to** violent combustion of the unburned mixture.

Connectors

Reason

∴ A, B **As a result of** increased pressure, the refrigerant condenses.

Sequence

A → B The pressure drops. The refrigerant is **now** returned to the evaporator.

Reference

The latter is | a coiled pipe | **mounted** in the freezer compartment.

| Heat |, **given off** by burning fuel particles, causes adjacent particles to ignite.

Selected Vocabulary

temperature control:

process verbs	process nouns	component
evaporate (-d)	evaporation	evaporator
compress (-ed)	compression	compressor
condense (-d)	condensation	condensor
refrigerate (-d)	refrigeration	refrigerator
expand (-ed)	expansion	
extract (-ed)	extraction	extractor

give off (given)
draw (drawn)
spread (spread)

properties:

flammable (= inflammable)
non-flammable

toxic (= poisonous)
non-toxic (= non-poisonous)

Unit 23

Presentation

Read the text. Number the tables and figure below and give them a title.

Hardening plain carbon steel:

The hardening of plain carbon steel consists of two stages; first heating to a specific temperature and then cooling rapidly. The cooling process is known as quenching. The correct temperature to which steel must be heated varies with its carbon content (see Fig. 23.1). Overheating can cause grain growth, resulting in weak components.

The hardness of the heat-treated steel depends on two factors:

1 Type of quenching bath
This contains either water or quenching oil, depending on the speed of cooling required. The more rapidly a plain carbon steel is cooled, the harder it is. However, overrapid cooling can result in faults, e.g. cracking and distortion. Therefore, the correct quenching bath should be chosen to treat the workpiece as required (see Table 23.2).

2 The carbon content (see Table 23.1).

Carbon content of steel	Effect of hardening
0.0 – 0.25%	No effect
0.3 – 0.5%	Some effect: becomes tougher
0.5 – 0.9%	Good effect: becomes hard
0.9 – 1.3%	Very good effect: becomes very hard

a. ----

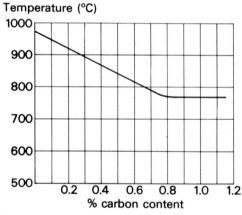

c. ----

% carbon content	Quenching bath	Required treatment
0.3 – 0.5	Oil	Toughening
0.5 – 0.9	Oil	Toughening
0.5 – 0.9	Water	Hardening
0.9 – 1.3	Oil	Hardening

b. ----

Practice 1

Use Fig. 23.1 and Table 23.1 to match the probable causes (in the box) with the faults indicated in Table 23.3.

	Carbon content of component	Process used	Fault
1	1.1%	Heated to 780°C. Quenched in water for hardening	Cracking of component
2	0.8%	Heated to 900°C. Quenched in water for hardening	Grain growth Weak component
3	0.4%	Heated to 850°C. Quenched in water for toughening	Distortion of component
4	0.7%	Heated to 950°C. Quenched in water for toughening	Grain growth and cracking

Table 23.3

Causes

Overheating
The use of water for quenching
The use of oil for quenching

1 Cracking of the component is probably caused by ____.

2 Grain growth causing a weak component is probably due to ____.

3 Distortion of the component is probably caused by ____.

4 Grain growth and cracking are probably due to ____.

Practice 2

Use Fig. 23.1, Table 23.1 and Table 23.2 to recommend the correct carbon content, heating temperature and type of quenching bath for the following requirements:

Requirements	% carbon content	Maximum temp. °C	Quenching bath
1 Very hard plain carbon steel component			
2 Hard plain carbon steel component			
3 Tough plain carbon steel component			

Table 23.4

Development

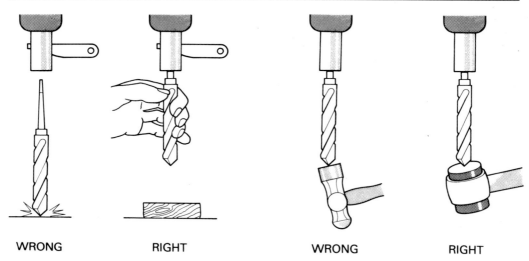

WRONG   RIGHT   WRONG   RIGHT

Figure 23.2 Avoiding drill damage

Use the text to complete Table 23.5:

A damaged drill point is a very common fault in the drilling process. It can be caused either by dropping the drill onto a hard surface when removing the drill from the spindle or by using a hard-faced hammer when inserting the drill. A damaged drill point can result in rough holes. These may also be caused by too rapid a feed or insufficient coolant.

Damaged corners, another common fault, may also occur for these last two reasons. Bluntness or incorrect grinding are probable causes of a broken drill. Broken drills may also be due to an insecurely clamped workpiece or jamming of the drill in the hole as a result of worn corners.

All faults of this kind can be avoided if the drill is kept in good condition and used correctly.

Failure/fault	Probable causes	Remedy
Damaged drill point	a. b.	
Rough holes	a. b. c.	
Damaged corners	a. b.	
A broken drill	a. b. c. d.	

Table 23.5 Fault-finding chart

Summary

Sentence Patterns

Overheating **can result in** faults.
Overheating **can cause** grain growth.

Damaged corners **may occur** *for several reasons.*
Broken drills **may be due to** jamming of the drill.

Grain growth **is** *probably* **caused** by overheating.

Selected Vocabulary

processes:

  quenching
  toughening

faults:

causes	effects
overheating	grain growth
overrapid cooling	cracking and distortion
overrapid feed	damage to drill points
insufficient cooling	damage to drill points
incorrect grinding	drill breakage
insecure clamping	drill breakage
bluntness	drill breakage

useful verbs:

grind (ground)	distort (-ed)
clamp (-ed)	damage (-d)
grow (grown)	break (broken)
crack (-ed)	avoid (-ed)
depend (-ed)	require (-d)
treat (-ed)	choose (chosen)
quench (-ed)	insert (-ed)

Unit 24

Presentation

Read the text and then complete Table 24.1:

Petrol will not burn unless it is mixed with air: normally the proportion of air to petrol required to burn fuel completely is 15 (air):1 (petrol). This means that 1 kg of petrol should be mixed with 15 kg of air. More air or less petrol gives a weak mixture i.e. an air:petrol ratio greater than 15:1. Less air or more petrol gives a rich mixture i.e. an air:petrol ratio of less than 15:1.

A weak mixture, which will mean very slow combustion, will result in high fuel consumption, low engine power and possibly overheating of the engine. A rich mixture, which will also mean slow combustion, will similarly result in high fuel consumption and low engine power. A further indication of a rich mixture is black or sooty exhaust gas.

Mixture strength	Combustion	Exhaust gas	Effects
Very weak, e.g. ____	____		____
Very rich, e.g. ____	____	____	____

Table 24.1

Practice 1

Use Table 24.1 to complete this text:

High fuel consumption and low engine power can be caused by either ____ or ____. If the exhaust gas is black, this will indicate ____. If the engine overheats, this will probably mean the mixture is too ____.

Now use the text above and Fig. 24.1 to complete the text on the next page:

White deposits and damaged porcelain insulation indicating overheating.

Excessive black deposits caused by an over-rich mixture.

Mild white deposits and electrode burnt indicating too weak a mixture.

Figure 24.1 Sparking plug conditions

Unit 24

Damage to sparking plugs can be caused by ____, ____, or ____. If the sparking plug has ____ and ____, this will ____. If the sparking plug ____. If ____.

Practice 2

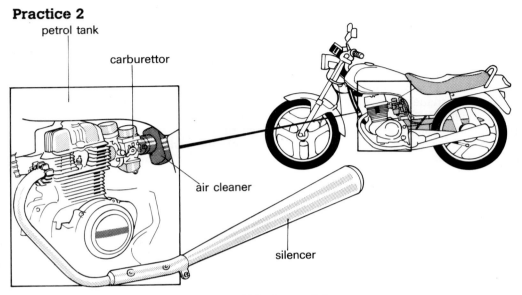

petrol tank

carburettor

air cleaner

silencer

Figure 24.2 A motorbike

Use Table 24.2 to complete the text:

Excessive fuel consumption can be caused by one of the following reasons: a choked air cleaner, ____, ____ or ____. If the air cleaner is not choked, examine the carburettor, since high fuel consumption could indicate either ____ or ____.

Check and tighten all screws and adjust as necessary. If, after checking the carburettor, fuel consumption is still high, it will probably mean ____.

Low engine power ____ by a weak mixture. A weak mixture ____ that the float needle is stuck, in which case remove the float needle and clean it.

If, after ____, engine power is still low, this ____ that there is an air leak at the carburettor joint. In this case ____.

Fault	Reasons	Remedy
Excessive fuel consumption	Choked air cleaner	Clean air cleaner
	Leaking carburettor	Check and tighten screws
	Incorrectly adjusted carburettor	Adjust as necessary
	Incorrect type of silencer	Fit correct silencer
Low engine power	Weak mixture due to jammed float needle	Remove float needle and clean
	Weak mixture due to air leak at carburettor joint	Check and tighten all screws

Table 24.2 Fault-finding chart